Muslim Palestine

Muslim Palestine

The Ideology of Ḥamās

Andrea Nüsse

ROUTLEDGE
RoutledgeCurzon
Taylor & Francis Group

Transferred to Digital Printing 2002
by RoutledgeCurzon, 11 New Fetter Lane
London EC4P 4EE

RoutledgeCurzon is an imprint of the Taylor & Francis Group

Printed in Great Britain by Hobbs the Printers Ltd, Totton, Hants

---

British Library Cataloguing in Publication Data

Nusse, Andrea
Muslim Palestine: the ideology of Hamas
1. Harakat al-Muqawamah al-Islamiyah 2. Ideology – Palestine – Religious aspects – Islam 3. Islamic fundamentalism
4. Jewish-Arab relations 5. Palestine – Politics and government – 1948–
I. Title
297.8′ 095694

ISBN 90-5702-334-2 (Softcover)

Contents

Le diable parait bien pâle
auprès de celui qui *dispose*
d'une vérité, de *sa* vérité.

Cioran

Glossary

Ahl al-kitāb: "The people of the Book". Muhammad referred to Jews and the Christians as such, distinguishing them from heathens, on account of their possessing divine books of revelation. Although they transmitted this revelation in a false way, the acceptance of the books was seen to give them a privileged position above followers of other religions. After their submission, they were granted free worship against payment of a poll-tax. An agreement ensured them the protection of the Muslim authorities.Violence of this defence alliance is considered a perfidy.

Bātil: Futile, vain, unreal, ungodly as opposed to the real (*ḥaqq*) as designed by God.

Bayān(āt): Declaration, statement. Here, the handouts of *Ḥamās* which are written and distributed in the Territories. They contain information about the movement's position, as well as about strike days and demonstrations.

Fiqh: Jurisprudence in Islam. All aspects of public and private life should be regulated by laws recognised by religion; the science of these laws is *fiqh*.

Ḥadīth: Tradition. Particularly, a record of actions or sayings of the Prophet and his companions which were originally transmitted through oral instruction.

Ḥamās: Acronym of Islamic Resistance Movement (*Ḥarakat al muqāwama al-Islāmiyya*) also meaning "zeal", "ardour" in Arabic. The movement was formed as one "wing" within the Muslim Brotherhood after the outbreak of the Palestinian uprising in December 1987. It was designed as a vehicle to mobilize support and to compete with the threat posed by fringe Islamic groups like the *Islamic Jihād*, as well as by the nationalist groups engaged in resistance to the Israeli occupation. *Ḥamās* rapidly developed into a full-fledged political movement, overshadowing its parent organisation and participating in the armed struggle through its own underground wing, the Al-Qassam Brigades. It also succeeded in developing a well organized and effective network of social services which extended from universities, to health centers and youth clubs. Combined with politicial pragmatism and flexibility, this Islamist movement soon became the main rival to the PLO competing for Palestinian leadership.

Ḥanīf: Used for those who possess the true and real religion, especially Abraham.

Ḥaqq: One of the names of God in Islam. Means the real, godly.

Islamic Jihād: (*al-Jihād al-Islāmī*) The second most influential Islamist movement (behind *Ḥamās*) in Palestine. Amid discontent with the reformational methods of the Muslim Brotherhood, political cells were created as early as 1979 in the Occupied Territories and especially in Gaza, the movement's stronghold. As an underground organisation, the movement has no open popular following, its membership remains selected and elitist. The *Islamic Jihād* was the first contemporary Islamist movement in Palestine which took up armed action against Israel and thus played a direct role in triggering off the *Intifāḍa* in 1987. Since the foundation of *Ḥamās* in late 1987 or 1988, the movement's political influence declined considerably. The organisation rejects the Peace Accords on religious grounds and continues armed operations against Israel, but never developed a broader political outlook.

Intifāḍa: The Palestinian uprising against the Israeli occupation that started in December 1987 and formally ended with the Peace Accords between Israel and the Palestinians in September 1993.

Jāhiliyya: Ignorance. Meaning the pagan times which reigned on the Arabian peninsula before the arrival of Muhammad. The theoretician of the Muslim Brotherhood, Sayyid Qutb, reinterpreted it as a situation which occurs at any time when God's programme and laws are neglected by society and rulers. Thus, most contemporary Muslim societies were considered by him to live in a state of *jāhiliyya*.

Jihād: Effort, striving. Generally known as holy war to spread Islam on earth. However, in many fundamentalist interpretations it means the personal striving to be a good Muslim, to raise children in an Islamic way.

Kāfir (ūn): Infidel(s). First applied to the Meccans who endeavoured to refute and revile the Prophet. The unbelievers were threatened with punishment and hell.

Kufr: Unbelief.

Mīthāq: Covenant, agreement, treaty, charter. Here, the convenant of *Ḥamās*, first circulated in August 1988, which laid down the main ideological and theoretical outlook of the movement.

Mujāhid(ūn) (Mujaheddin): Fighter participating in *Jihād*.

Muslim Brotherhood: The parent organisation of all Sunni fundamentalist movements in Palestine. Founded in Egypt in 1928 by Hasan al-Banna, it politicised Islam by calling for the creation of an Islamic state and soon set up branches in various Arab countries. The Palestinian branch followed a reformational approach aiming at a reform of Palestinian society from within, insisting on Islamic education and social work. It fought the secularism of the PLO, but not the Israeli occupation. It did not react to the growing popular discontent and impatience with Israeli occupation which culminated in the creation of *Islamic Jihād* in 1979 by dissident Brotherhood members. Only with the outbreak of the *Intifāḍa* in December 1987 did the Muslim Brotherhood recognise the growing gap between its quietistic, apolitical approach and the longing of the Palestinian people for more combative and militant action; as a consequence *Ḥamās* was founded.

Qur'ān: The sacred book of the Muslims, containing the collected revelations of the Prophet Muhammad in definitive written form.

Tafsīr: Commentaries of the *Qur'ān:* and the science of interpreting the sacred book.

Umma: The Qur'anic word for community, people. Here, generally meaning the Muslim people that are the objects of the divine plan of salvation.

Introduction

Islamic fundamentalism can be seen daily in the headlines of the Western media. It is often presented in a simplified way as a backward-looking religious movement whose main enemies are Western culture and Western political systems. Intellectuals and scientists of many different academic disciplines have written about this phenomenon; often characterizing it as a "fight against modernity"[1], or as facets of a "regressive" religion incapable of change[2]. Was the rise of Islamic fundamentalism inevitable because "la forme d'expression qui vient le plus naturellement aux musulmans pour exprimer leur contestation et leurs aspirations est religieuse"?[3] Islamists would probably agree with this statement. They blame today's Muslims for neglecting Islamic values and practices. But such assertions about the "nature" of people and their religious life cannot be taken for granted – no matter whether they come from fundamentalists or orientalists.

I would agree with Sami Zubaida's general definition of the varieties of Islamic fundamentalism as referring to "modern political movements and ideas, mostly oppositional, which seek to establish, in one sense or another, an Islamic state"[4]. In the so-called fundamentalist interpretation Islam becomes narrowed down to a political doctrine that is considered the only source of reference in politics and society. Despite different claims, Islam has not developed proper political concepts, but it is true nevertheless that the emphasis on its communal solidarity may have favoured a political outlook of Islam throughout history. Modern fundamentalists sharpen this political aspect of the religion and try to make it the dominating interpretation. Islam has been part of the politics of the 20th century as a source for official legitimation as well as in oppositional populist movements such as the Muslim Brotherhood. Politics based on Islam are no simple product of some essential, historically given body of beliefs and practices, but the result of particular constructions of religious discourses related to current situations. This does not question the fact that the religious discourse is shaped by and largely based on traditional Islamic ideas and concepts. How those are used and transformed in the political struggle is the subject of this study which analyses the ideology of one group identified with "Islamic Fundamentalism", that of the Islamic Resistance Movement in Palestine or *Ḥamās*.[5] It is hoped that in concentrating in detail on this group, many of the generalizations so prevalent today can be avoided. Despite the public attention paid to *Ḥamās* since the outbreak of the *Intifāḍa* in December 1987, not enough is known about the movement's ideology and its use of historical and contemporary sources.[6] This task is all the more important if we want to anticipate future developments. My working hypothesis here is that *Ḥamās* is a modern political movement involved in a struggle for power, whose oppositional discourse is based on religious references. It is a national organization that is surprisingly pragmatic and clear-sighted in its analysis of international politics. Despite the repetitive use of supposedly fixed concepts, it demonstrates an impressive ideological flexibility. This work will stress, for example, the comparatively strong nationalistic and democratic elements in *Ḥamās*' ideology. It will also highlight the eclectic and pragmatic use of traditional Islamic sources of a political and social movement that refutes common social scientific portrayals, attempts at global classification as well as the self-characterizations of Islamists themselves.

Study of the ideology of *Ḥamās* seems all the more important in the light of recent history. After the decision of the Israeli President, Benjamin Netanjahu, in March 1997 to build a new settlement in East-Jerusalem on a hill called Har Homa, cutting Arab Jerusalem almost entirely from its Palestinian hinterland, the peace process almost came to an end. A mini-*Intifāḍa* is developing and with the attack on a café in Tel Aviv, suicide bombings are starting up again. In the international political community and the media, *Ḥamās* is once again considered no more than a terrorist group.[7] But despite acts of political violence, the movement remains the main political opposition to the Palestine Liberation Organization (PLO) and Yassir Arafat, the head of the Palestinian National Authority (PNA) in the Gaza Strip and the West Bank. The provocative Israeli policy is strengthening the position and support of *Ḥamās* that virulently opposes the peace process.[8] As a whole, *Ḥamās* remains the strongest rival to secular-nationalist Palestinian politics and should be taken seriously as such. Israel and the PLO should know by now that there cannot be a stable settlement without taking account of the Islamic factor whose most important representative is *Ḥamās* with its various wings.[9]

In this work, I will analyze the system of thought and ideas of this main Islamic group in the Territories, as it is expressed in certain Arabic language publications. I thus focus on the purely ideological side of the phenomenon: How do *Ḥamās*-activists see the conflict with Israel and with what arguments do they oppose peace negotiations? How do they explain the present crisis of the Arab-Islamic world and how do they view its future? What is their attitude towards the West? Which parts of the Qur'ān and of Islamic theoretical literature (biographical literature and *Ḥadīth*) do they use, what is their interpretation of those teachings and how do they apply it to the present situation? Do they use modern concepts and ideas of Western or other non-Islamic origin? If this is the case, by which mechanisms do they integrate them into their own ideological framework? In a second step I will describe how these basic principles and methods of thought are applied to specific events in the region.

I am neither looking at the structure of the movement nor at the composition of its constituency. Despite the justified criticism of classic Orientalist methods, I am not afraid of the old-fashioned *Ideengeschichte*. Orientalist criticism seems to have led, unfortunately, to a neglect of the study of texts. But if the writings are not mistaken for reality and the research is not guided by the wish to provide any ahistorical proof of some "essence of Islam" – as often was the case in the past – then this "Orientalist" type of work can be an important supplement, if not a solid basis for any more contextual research.

As *Ḥamās* developed from the Palestinian Muslim Brotherhood and is largely based on their framework of thought, the valuable material that already exists about the history of the Brotherhood in the Occupied Territories is highly relevant to this study. However, the policies and actions of *Ḥamās* mark a major change from previous Muslim Brotherhood politics. Until the outbreak of the *Intifāḍa*, the Brotherhood had not actively participated in the resistance against the Israeli occupation. It had focused on the "traditional" fundamentalist activities of religious education and moral purification of the society from the inside. This departure from classical Muslim Brotherhood activities in the Territories must be sought in the ideology of *Ḥamās* and the latter therefore deserves specific attention.

There has been a lot more research on the structure, organisation and the history of the *Ḥamās*-movement, but it lacks a satisfactory analysis of the movement's system of beliefs. The passages about ideology are often exclusively based on the convenant, the *Mīthāq*, which gives the broad theoretical outline of the movement, but fails to give any information about the application of these general ideas. Furthermore, a number of articles have been published about the ideological position of *Ḥamās* on specific points such as *Jihād* or the peace negotiations. But while these articles provide illumination on these specific points, they fail to fit particular *Ḥamās*' positions into the movement's *Weltanschauung*; they fail to give a comprehensive idea of precisely this world-view.

Through the elaboration and analysis of *Ḥamās'* global worldview and then the application of it to specific events in the region, I hope to show the techniques of elaborating a position on the basis of certain supposedly fixed religious principles and the procedure of departing from them when necessary. Those capacities and techniques are crucial to the future development of the movement which has been confronted with radical changes since the Declaration of Principles in 1993. While the written material used for this analysis mainly dates from 1990 to 1992 – years in which *Ḥamās* elaborated its specific ideology and became a mass movement – these mechanisms of developing and adapting an ideology to changing political circumstances are of still greater relevance today. Source material up to 1996 is used in the second part of the book.

The main sources for this research are the *Mīthāq*, the journal *Filasṭīn al-Muslima*, which could be described as the unofficial organ of *Ḥamās*, as well as the handbills of the movement, published on a day-to-day basis in the Territories. The *Mīthāq* was first circulated in August 1988 and lays down the main theoretical and ideological outlook of the Islamic Resistance Movement. It is interpreted as an Islamic alternative to the political blueprints of the secular nationalists.[10] *Ḥamās* claims that the Qur'ān is its constitution. The organization therefore interpreted the Qur'ānic ideas in order to clarify their position in the present struggle.[11] The journal *Filasṭīn al-Muslima*, like many Arab publications (fundamentalist or secularist nature alike) is published in the West. It was first produced in Manchester, now in London. Issued every two months since 1982, it became a monthly journal in April 1990. Frisch reveals that it is published by the "Islamic League of Palestinian Youth".[12] He confirms that it is the major and most consistent publication brought out by the Palestinian branch of the Muslim Brotherhood and had consequently become the spokesman "of sorts" for *Ḥamās*.[13] Thus *Filasṭīn al-Muslima* regularly publishes the *bayānāt* (handbills) of *Ḥamās* issued inside the Territories, as well as long interviews with leaders of the organization. Repeatedly we can read acknowledgements of the Muslim Brotherhood and its participation in the struggle to liberate Palestine. The fact that in May 1996 the editors denied speaking officially on behalf of *Ḥamās* does not change my assessment. They did so after being accused of calling for terrorist acts after the arrest of *Ḥamās*-leader Abu Marzuq in the United States.[14] In order to avoid persecution after the wave of bomb attacks carried out by *Ḥamās*-activists in Israel at the beginning of the year, the journalists have distanced themselves from the movement in order not to endanger the publication. Still, the way they do so clearly indicates the strong affiliation between *Filasṭīn al-Muslima* and *Ḥamās*, the strongest Islamic movement in the Occupied Territories and the autonomous regions. "The magazine is honoured to support this movement and with it all movements that fight the occupation."[15] The attacks of *Ḥamās* and others are "in our eyes no terrorist acts, but part of a legitimate resistance"[16], and "our support of Hamas and Islamic Jihad is the expression of our conviction that we defend a national liberation movement fighting occupation."[17]

Since that time, the editors always talk about *Ḥamās* and "Islamic Jihad" in the same breath whereas before only *Ḥamās* was mentioned. Furthermore the editors do not publish the *Ḥamās*-handbills verbatim, but summarise them in their own words. But as most of the source material used in this work dates from before 1996, there is no doubt that the journal expressed in an unfiltered manner the views of *Ḥamās*.

At the same time, it is interesting that the journalists producing the journal are not the same people who publish the *bayānāt* of *Ḥamās* inside the Territories. The journalists, mainly living in Great Britain, are constantly exposed to the influences of a Western society. The quality of political analysis suggests they have a good education. This level of sophistication is in contrast to the handbills of *Ḥamās*. No doubt this difference is also due to the different purposes of each publication. While the *bayānāt* serve mainly to mobilise the Palestinian population, announcing strike days and other forms of action, the journal serves to provide analysis and background information in a more global context and to clarify theoretical principles. Both publications can and must be seen as complementing each other. *Filasṭīn al-Muslima* can be considered a uniquely important source for the study of *Ḥamās*' ideology.[18] I should specify that the source material was chosen for its interest with regard to the Palestine conflict, therefore it is more telling about the political outlook of *Ḥamās* than about the movement's social agenda, even though both domains cannot properly be separated.

I will first give a short overview of the development of Islamic thought in the 20th century. Though I concentrate on the ideological side of the subject, this will nevertheless be followed by a short overview of the main socio-economic developments in the Territories and the transformation of Palestinian society during the *Intifāḍa*, since this period is the focus of this study. However, I do not claim to establish any concrete link between both domains. In the following chapters, I will describe and analyse the ideas and concepts of *Ḥamās*, arranged according to the pattern of thought revealed in the texts. Starting from the main problem (the existence of Israel, the Jews and Judaism) and the goal (establishment of an Islamic state in Palestine) proceeding to the feeling of urgency (illustrated by the example of the mass immigration of Soviet Jews) and the perceived isolation of Muslims on the political stage (in the international, Arab and Palestinian arena), I will come to the proposed means for achieving the stated goal (*Jihād* in the form of *Intifāḍa* and democratization in the Arab world). This is followed by some other major aspects of the ideology (such as views of minorities and the West). In the second part of this book I will see how these convictions and general principles of thought are applied to specific events. It is organised chronologically and should serve as an illustration of the ideas brought out in Part One. Only where *Ḥamās* departs from fixed principles or further elaborates ideological positions will I go into deeper analysis. The impression of redundancy at certain points is due to the repetitive character of *Ḥamās*' statements. The chosen events are the second Gulf War, the peace negotiations that started in Madrid, the mass deportation of Islamists to South Lebanon, the Declaration of Principles and the massacre in Hebron. In Chapter Sixteen I will look at the position of *Ḥamās* towards the Palestine National Authority (PNA) as the initiation of state-building demands the biggest effort in reformulating and adapting positions after Oslo. This chapter will be followed by an outlook on the future political development of *Ḥamās*. In the conclusion I will summarise and assess the formation of ideology.

Before proceeding I should examine the matter of terminology. The commonly-used terms "Islamic Fundamentalism", "Islamic Revivalism" or "Islamism" with their various connotations do not necessarily reveal what I am talking about. Hodgson asserted that "the story of scholarly achievement can almost be summed up in successive refinements of terminology."[19] Unfortunately, scholarship has not picked up the refined terminology for Islamic studies put forward by Hodgson.[20] Thus we still use the term "Islam" while speaking about such different things as religious cult, society or the culture and symbols associated with a religion.

A similar dilemma is encountered by scholars if they want to speak about the contemporary phenomenon of Islamic movements. Are they best described as "fundamentalist", "neo-fundamentalist", "Islamist" or "revivalist"? These terms indeed appear inadequate and misleading. As Sami Zubaida points out, all Islam is fundamentalist in the sense that its ultimate validity is based on the recognised canonical sources such as the Qur'ān and the Sunna of the Prophet.[21] This discussion about terminology could be the subject of an entire work. As I want to move on to examine what these terms hide, I will only say that the terms can be adequate if they are at first defined. Consequently I will use the two terms "fundamentalist" and "Islamist" in this work – not least in order to avoid tiresome and stylistically awkward repetition. Both are used only in reference to the Islamic Resistance Movement in the Occupied and partly Autonomous Territories. The use of the two terms seems justified because both highlight different aspects of the ideology I am discussing. It is "fundamentalist" in the sense that the Qur'ān, the Sunna and the way of life of the early Muslim community are taken as the yardstick for truth and thought, and as the model for action and behavior. It is "Islamist" in the sense that it Islamises and thus incorporates modern concepts and ideas that are often of Western origin. Hopefully, the reader will have a clearer idea about the nature of this thought and thus the adequate terminology at the end of the book.

For the English quotes of the Qur'ān the translation by M.M. Khatib, *The Bounteous Koran. A translation of Meaning and Commentary*, (London, 1986) which is authorized by Al-Azhar was used. The journal *Filasṭīn al-Muslima* will be referred to in the notes as FM. The transliteration of Arabic words – with the exception of those well known by the Western reader – was done according to the system used in the *International Journal of Middle Eastern Studies*. Arabic names are generally given in their English version.

At this point I want to express my gratitude to Ron Nettler who first encouraged me to start this ambitious project when I was a student at Oxford and then followed its development with further advice and support while I worked as a Middle East editor for the daily newspaper "Der Tagesspiegel" in Berlin.

NOTES

1. Thomas Meyer, *Fundamentalismus – Aufstand gegen die Moderne*, (Hamburg 1989).
2. Jean-Claude Barreau, *De L'Islam en général et du monde moderne en particulier*, Le Pré aux clercs, (Paris, 1991), p. 32.
3. Bernhard Lewis in his foreword to Gilles Kepel, *Le Prophète et le Pharaon. Les Movements Islamiques dans l'Egypte Contemporaine*, (Paris, 1984), p. 16.
4. Sami Zubaida, "The Quest for the Islamic State: Islamic Fundamentalism in Egypt and Iran", p. 38. In: Zubaida, *Islam, the People and the State*, (London, 1989), pp. 38–63.
5. *Ḥamās* is the acronym of *ḥarikat al-muqāwama al-islāmiyya*. At the same time the Arabic word signifies "zeal, ardor".
6. The author has made a first attempt to fill this gap with the article "The Ideology of *Ḥamās*: Palestinian Islamic Fundamentalist Thought on the Jews, Israel and Islam", in: Ronald Nettler (ed), *Studies in Muslim-Jewish Relationship*, vol. 1 (Amsterdam, 1993), pp. 97–125.
7. The attack was executed by a Palestinian close to *Ḥamās*, but not claimed by the movement. See *Middle East International*, no. 547, 4 April 1997, p. 3.

8. Following the Har Homa crisis *Ḥamās* won elections in two former strongholds of Fataḥ, in the Employees Union at Najah University and the Engineers Association in the Gaza Strip. See *Middle East International*, no. 547, 4 April 1997, p. 4.
9. The Islamic Resistance Movement is as little a monolithic bloc as any other political movement.
10. Hillel Frisch, "The Case of Religious Emulation: The Nationalization of Universal Religious Doctrine in the Palestinian Fundamentalist Movement", p. 23. In: *Middle East Focus*, Fall 1990, vol. 13 (3), pp. 18–25.
11. *Mīthāq Ḥamās*, p. 9.
12. Frisch, op. cit., p. 21.
13. Ibid.
14. FM, May 1996, editorial p. 2.
15. Ibid. *Ḥamās* is meant by "this movement".
16. Ibid.
17. Ibid.
18. The editors complained that for many years *Filasṭīn al-Muslima* had only been available to readers in the Arab world by subscription, as the publication was not authorised in most Arab countries. But the recent "climate of opening" in the Arab "homeland" (*waṭan*) allowed progress in this respect. In March 1990 the monthly could, for the first time, be sold legally in Jordan. The 1000 issues delivered were sold in a record time and an additional 1000 issues were ordered immediately. The issue April 1990 was the first one to be distributed in the Saudi market.
19. Marshall G.S. Hodgson, *The Venture of Islam. Conscience and History in a World Civilization*, Vol. I, (Chicago, 1974), p. 46
20. For Hodgson's definition of the terms Islam, Islamdom, Islamicate, Islamic, see ibid, pp. 58ff.
21. Sami Zubaida, "Islam,Cultural Nationalism and the Left", p. 2. In: *Review of Middle East Studies*, 4 (1988), pp. 1–32.

CHAPTER ONE

The Context

DEVELOPMENT OF ISLAMIC THOUGHT IN THE 20TH CENTURY

The history of Islamic thought since the second half of the 19th century is intrinsically linked to the history of Western expansion. Western dominance of the Arab-Muslim world and the indigenous reaction against it, are the main factors that shaped modern Islamic thought. Western dominance on the military and economic levels was accompanied by attacks on the cultural identity of the Arab-Muslim world. This was brought about by the importation of Western intellectual concepts in general, and by the insistence on the *mission civilisatrice* of the West, which was justified by a description of non-European peoples and religions as backward and inferior.

These numerous attacks on Arab-Muslim society forced the main trends of Islamic thought into a defensive position which it has found difficult to abandon. This point is absolutely essential for an understanding of contemporary intellectual development in the Arab-Muslim world.[1] As a consequence, subsequent Islamic thought has been marked by a more or less strongly developed apologetic character.[2] This characteristic has become a prominent feature of Islamic thought in the 20th century. It can also be found in today's fundamentalist thought which tries to be more assertive.

The Islamic discussion focused on the reasons for the relative backwardness and weakness of Arab-Muslim societies. Religious reform was perceived by many Arab thinkers as a tool for social and political change. One current of thought, represented by the Indian Sir Sayyid Ahmad Khan (1817–1898), advocated the uncritical adoption of Western concepts and institutions. An Islamic resistance to Western colonialism stood at the centre of Jamal al-Din al-Afghani's (1838/39–1897) thought and life. The Egyptian Muhammad Abduh (1849–1905) finally developed a reinterpretation of Islam which was extremely influential for subsequent reformism. In the first instance, Abduh's reforms were aimed at religious and educational institutions such as Al-Azhar.[3] In his view, archaic scholastic religiosity, as well as popular Islam, marked by magic and saint worship, had led to the present weakness of Islamic polities and societies. This development was by no means intrinsic to Islam; on the contrary, Islam had anticipated Western principles like democracy and equality.[4] Thus the revival of the "true" Islamic heritage, which had been corrupted for centuries, was the only way to end the crisis. Abduh defended Islam as a religion appealing to the believer's reason and allowed the believer to interpret the sacred texts symbolically if they seemed to contradict reason.[5] His basic reform was thus rational understanding and presentation of Islamic truth while remaining entirely within the Islamic tradition.[6]

Abduh shares with later fundamentalists an insistence on the need for a return to some sort of original Islam and an emphasis on education. But they differ in their attitude towards the West. Abduh regarded the West, despite its oppressive politics in the region, as a cultural model for strength and progress. His interpretation of Islam aimed to justify the adoption of concepts and models that were associated with Western societies. Later fundamentalist thinkers, on the other hand, rejected all values perceived as Western and did not differentiate between the political behaviour of the West and its intellectual achievements. They insisted on the differences between both civilisations while asserting their Islamic model.[7] Abduh exerted great intellectual influence which was translated into practical changes mainly in the sphere of education. But in contrast to later fundamentalists, his thought lacked the call for an Islamic state and government.[8] It was the Muslim Brotherhood that politicised Islam by calling for an Islamic state.

The Muslim Brotherhood, founded in 1928 in Egypt by Hasan al-Banna, been the most prominent fundamentalist current in Sunni

Islam in the Arab world. Influenced by the ideas of Abduh and his disciple Rashid Rida, it was launched as a movement for education and reform of "heart and mind".[9] But the movement soon developed a political dimension calling for an Islamic reform of state and government, where the existing order should be displaced by one based on Islamic law (*sharī'a*). This social and political Islamic order (*al-niẓām al-islāmī*) could be achieved by popular mobilisation. The Brotherhood thus became the first modern populist party in the Arab-Muslim world.[10] Based on systematic organisation and recruitment, its ideological-political appeal, accompanied by welfare programmes, was directed at the individual.[11] The Muslim Brotherhood also had a secret apparatus which was responsible for the assassination of politicians.[12] Initially linked to the Free Officers and the coup of 1952, the Muslim Brotherhood was soon declared illegal and its members persecuted. Only under Anwar al-Sadat was the organisation allowed to function legally again.[13] Under Banna's successor, Hasan al-Hudaiba, the movement lost its former coherence and conflicting factions were engaged in internal struggles. Out of this dissent developed the various fundamentalist groups that we find in Egypt and the rest of the Arab world today, many of whom take a more militant stance than the Muslim Brotherhood.[14] In line with its pan-Islamic ideology, the Muslim Brotherhood developed branches in other Arab countries. In addition to its establishment in Jordan, Iraq and Lebanon the movement played an important political role in Syria. In contrast to the Egyptian organisation, the Syrian Brethren defended parliamentary democracy and entered parliament in 1947.[15] Thus the battle for *al-niẓām al-islāmī* has taken different forms according to circumstances.

The most important intellectual and theoretician of the Muslim Brotherhood was Sayyid Qutb. The doctrine and methods developed and propagated by this author are still highly important for contemporary Sunni fundamentalist groups. In his early work *Social Justice in Islam* (*Al-'Adāla al-Ijtimā'iyya fī l-Islām*), Qutb demonstrates that Islam guarantees social justice which emanates from the Islamic principle of the equality of men.[16] Islamic rule thus excludes oppression which no man-made system such as communism or capitalism can avoid.[17]

But it is in the most influencial and voluminous Qur'anic exegesis (*tafsīr*) *Fī Ẓilāl al-Qur'ān*, written mainly in prison between 1953 and 1964 [18] that Qutb exposed his most novel ideas:[19] his interpretation of *Jāhiliyya* and the notion of *Ḥākimiyyat Allāh*. He does not limit *Jāhiliyya* to the time of pagan ignorance reigning on the Arabian peninsula before the arrival of Muhammad, but interprets it as a situation which occurs at any time when God's programme and laws are neglected by society and rulers.[20] Faith is not a mere belief, but has to be expressed in deeds and daily life. True Muslims must express their faith through active participation in the Islamic venture on earth. Societies with man-made legislation such as constitutions other than the Qu'rān are considered to live in *Jāhiliyya*.[21] Thus most of the existing governments in the Arab-Muslim world are considered *jāhilī* which represents a revolutionary departure from traditional Islamic teaching in which it is a serious infraction to declare a Muslim an infidel. This new interpretation provides Sunni Islamic thought with the ideological basis for opposition against Muslim governments. Thus Qutb's *Tafsīr* can accurately be described as a "commentary with a definite aim"[22] or a "campaign of struggle".[23] "His driving objective was that the Muslims of today should be able to live and practice true Islam in the same way as the early Islamic generations."[24]

Following the example of the first Muslims who emmigrated to Medina (*hijra*) and only attacked Mekka when they felt strong enough to do so, Qutb elaborated the theory of an ever growing nucleaus of "true" believers that should be developed until it can wage a *Jihād* against the surrounding society and its rulers. He believed that only through *Jihād* could the sovereinty of God (*ḥākimiyyat Allāh*) could be re-established. This would be achieved when the *Sharī'a* has become the only source of law. Qutb did not elaborate how exactly the state, society and economy would be organised under the Islamic order.

In contrast to Qutb, the Indian fundamentalist thinker Abu Ala al-Mawdudi developed a detailed blueprint for the organisation of an ideal Islamic state and built up the group "Jamī'a Islāmī", founded by him in 1941 in British India, along these lines.[25] In fact, Mawdudi had already developed the interpretation of *Jāhiliyya* which Qutb then made a major element of his analysis.[26] He is the author of the other important Qur'ān exegesis of the latter half of the 20th century.[27]

Islamic thought was only to come to the forefront of political debate after the Arab military defeat in the Six-Day-War in June 1967 which constituted a watershed in the contemporary history of the Arab-Muslim world. The "moral crisis"[28] that followed the defeat led to harsh self-criticism from the younger generation and the search for alternative paths. One current of thought criticised yesterday's radicals, Nasser and the Ba'th Party, as not having gone far enough. By limiting their revolutions to the strictly political level, they had capitulated to tradition, the arch-enemy of progress, in all other domains. These new radicals turned to the writings of Guevara, Debray, Marx, Giap and dreamed about a broad revolutionary movement including guerilla warfare. The channel for this revolution was supposed to be the Palestinian movement. Liberalism had become another word for colonialism and was discredited. Fouad Ajami shows that the political milieu had become less hospitable to liberal ideas and politics.[29]

The other response to the "moral crisis" was an Islamic one. As we have seen, the debate about the relation between Islam and the modern world had preoccupied the Arab world since the 19th century without coming to any final conclusion. Thus it was no surprise that the debate about Islam reemerged after the defeat of 1967. The Islamic current attributed the Muslims' defeat against the Western stronghold in the region, Israel, to the loss of faith. Using similiar arguments as the new radicals, these fundamentalists stated the need for an ideology to guide society. Their solution was a certain vision of Islam considered as an authentic, not imported, force. Authenticity again became the yardstick of thought.[30] What emerged was a populist and activist Islam as represented by Muhammad Jalal Kishk or the Muslim Brotherhood.

But in the first place more traditional Islam, which the Arab monarchies had used as a weapon against Nasser, triumphed. Saudi-Arabia had raised the banner of Islam in its struggle against Marxists and liberals – and could finally decide the power battle in its favour. In fear of an imminent revolution as advocated by the new radicals, Egypt entered an alliance with the traditional states. "The logic of the state system (...) asserted itself."[31] The defeat of the Palestinians in Jordan in 1970 marked the triumph of the dominant order. The Palestinian movement finally became institutionalised when the Palestinian Liberation Organisation (PLO) – pursuing the limited goal of statehood – was recognised in the Rabat Resolution 1974 as the "sole, legitimate representative" of the Palestinians. Thus the Palestinian movement was absorbed into the dominant order.

The 1973 war helped to diffuse frustration and radicalism. The Arab "victory" in the war and petrodollar-power that followed could be perceived as the beginning of a new era. The dependence on and domination by the West seemed for a brief period to belong to the past. Massive technological purchases and the aquisition of new skills determined the new rationality put forward by the Arab oil monarchies. But the expectations could not be met. The integration of the Arab-Muslim world into the Western dominated world-economy and world-society had failed again. The situation of the mass of the population, especially of the often university-educated younger generation, did not improve. Oppostion to the ruling elites and the dominating West emerged and drew upon the Sunni fundamentalist thought, as developed by the Muslim Brotherhood, Qutb and Mawdudi, for its ideology.

The revival of Islam in Palestine was influenced by the region-wide development described above. Still, each Islamist movement in the Arab world is marked by events and developments specific to the national framework in which it develops. In the case of Palestine, the defeat of the forces of the PLO in Lebanon in 1982 led to a situation of confusion and reorganisation that propelled political Islam to the forefront.[32] But only with the outbreak of the *Intifāḍa* in December 1987 did Islamism began to play a key role in Palestinian politics. The creation of *Ḥamās* under Sheikh Ahmed Yassin in December 1987 or early 1988[33] was the answer of the Muslim Brotherhood to the popular uprising against the Israeli occupation and marked the turning away from the quietist and reformist approach of the Brotherhood. As a highly politicised force *Ḥamās* quickly rose to prominence in the uprising and became a serious rival to the secular nationalist forces organised in the PLO.

FEATURES OF THE SOCIO-ECONOMIC DEVELOPMENT IN THE OCCUPIED TERRITORIES AND THE *INTIFĀḌA*

The socio-economic development of the Occupied Territories was intimately linked to the creation of the state of Israel and the nature of the Israeli occupation after 1967. The influx of large numbers of uprooted refugees into the West Bank and the Gaza Strip after the Arab-Israeli conflicts of 1948 and 1967 created new demographic conditions with greatly destabilizing effects. In 1987 the West Bank had, according to Israeli estimations, 860,000 inhabitants (excluding the 130,000 inhabitants of East-Jerusalem), of whom 381,000 were considered refugees.[34] The small Gaza Strip had officialy 560,000 inhabitants, of whom 454,000 were refugees. This is a population density of 3,754 people per square mile which is equivalent to Hong Kong's and among the highest in the world.[35] In 1984, about 46.6 percent of the total population of the West Bank was under 15 years old; in Gaza it was 47.8 percent. Projections of the population for the year 2002 indicate 1.5 million people in the West Bank and up to one million in the Gaza Strip, which would mean a growth rate of 43 percent and 55 percent respectively.[36] This picture can justly be described as a "human time bomb",[37] especially when seen against the background of poor facilities and a stagnant economic situation.

Since 1967, the dominating factor shaping the socio-economic development of the Occupied Territories has been the Israeli occupation. The occupation constituted "a web of all-embracing restrictions on the every-day activities" of the Palestinians.[38] The press was censored, freedom of movement restricted and curfews made Palestinian labourers working in Israel lose income and jobs. Export restrictions could change from one day to the other and ruin entrepreneurs. Property rights were precarious in the Occupied Territories where land was frequently expropriated for "public use" or military reasons. Military justice was applied and the verdicts were usually considered final. Schools and universities were regularly closed for long periods. Thus the sense of insecurity and instability were prevailing characteristics of the Palestinian population living under occupation. This is even more the case of the refugee population which lives in "permanently temporary conditions".[39]

The economic consequences of the occupation were profound and led to important social and political changes in society. The main result has been the lack of economic development in terms of structural transformation.[40] The low levels of government investment in social and economic infrastructure in the Gaza Strip, tax laws discriminating against the Palestinian producer, restrictions on access to foreign markets, as well as on the creation of industrial zones, unions, research and training facilities, prohibitions on the development of credit facilities were some of the Israeli policies undermining the ability of Gazan economy to create the infrastructure required for sustained economic growth. Generally speaking, these factors also applied to the West Bank economy.[41]

The most important structural change due to the occupation was the emergence of a significant sector of mainly unskilled or semiskilled wage labourers working in Israeli enterprises such as construction, agriculture and the service sector.[42] This trend away from employment in agriculture, which was until 1967 the mainstay of the West Bank economy and an important export earner for the Gaza Strip, was the direct result of Israeli expropriation of land on a large scale either for military reasons or for Jewish settlements. Furthermore, Israeli water policies have prevented Palestinian farmers from expanding irrigation and put water use under strict control. At the same time, there were approximately 65,000 Jewish settlers living in the West Bank and some 2,700 in the Gaza Strip[43] who are not restricted in their use of water and even have the right to drill new wells.[44] These illegal settlements[45] underlined the Israeli intention to create "des faits accomplis" and contributed strongly to Palestinian frustration.[46]

The masses of wage labourers who daily crossed the Green Line to work in Israel had even closer contact with the Jewish society which often exploited and humiliated them. They were continually made aware of the contrast between the quality of life on the two sides of the Green Line. As the Palestinians from the Territories were not allowed to enter Unions inside Israel, they remained unorganized and took unpopular, menial jobs that Israelis did not want. Officially employed people had to pay about 30 percent of their wages in taxes and social security payments without generally being entitled to the benefits available to an Israeli worker. At the bottom of the labour scale were those men who sought work on a daily basis. They go to gathering points known as "slave markets"[47] where contractors pick out workers from the crowd. As the Gazan working class is totally dependent on the Israeli market and the fluctuations of its economy, Palestinian labourers live in a permanent state of uncertainty and anxiety.[48]

Most other social groups suffered under Israeli occupation, the difference was in degree. Large land owners lost the large feudal estates that represented the basis for a feudalist system and often got engaged in trade.[49] But the restriction of trade markets and a 15 percent value tax imposed by Israel weakened the merchants as well. After 1967 Israel closed the European and East-European markets for Gazan citrus fruit. Since the occupation, most agricultural exports went to Jordan and thence to the Arab world. Generally the bridges over the Jordan have been kept open for goods, but they were sometimes closed for political reasons or punishment which results in unpredictable losses for farmers.[50] Israel was determined not to allow products from the Territories to compete with its own highly subsidised agricultural products which were dumped on the markets in the Territories.[51] Special permits for the import of certain Palestinian products could be cancelled without notice according to the need of the Israeli economy.[52] Hence instability and anxiety also reigned in this social strata.

Faced with the loss of land as a means of livelihood, education was often the only investment left for Palestinians and constituted the main means of social ascent, including the possibility of emigration. This explains why almost one third of the Palestinian population are students.[53] But the economic and political developments in the Arab countries made Palestinian work emigration more difficult. Most of the academic qualifications cannot be used within the largely stagnant economies of the Territories.[54]

Even though the traditional social hierarchy was strongly eroded by the economic transformations under occupation, no clear new class structure emerged in the Occupied Territories. In the West Bank the village society no longer presented a hierarchy of power based on the ownership of land.[55] At the same time, the full proletarization of the wage labour force was prevented as land and family ties remained in place because Palestinians were not allowed to settle down in the Israeli towns they worked in.

The last important aspect of life in the Territories was the constant denial of Palestinian identity by Israel. This "central theme of Israel's policy towards the Palestinians"[56], which Noam Chomsky called "cultural genocide"[57], came clearly to the fore in the domain of education. As Israeli authorities supervised the Palestinian educational system, they baned books with references to Palestine as an Arab territory or to Palestinian identity as translated in Palestinian poetry or literature for example.[58] In the UNRWA schools which provided education for

47 percent of the pupils in Gaza Strip and for nine percent in the West Bank[59] no attempt was made to develop a Palestinian curriculum.[60] In the West Bank these schools used the Jordanian curriculum, in the Gaza Strip the Egyptian one.

The *Intifāḍa*, which broke out in December 1987, was the result of these developments stretching over more than 20 years. The uprising brought some trends in Palestinian society to the fore that had been evident for years. Schiff and Ya'ari analyze the *Intifāḍa* as the "rebellion of the poor" and the "outburst by the forsaken and forgotten at the bottom of the social heap".[61] The depressing living conditions resulting from Israel's economic policies in the Territories were the real driving forces behind the radicalization of the Palestinians and constituted the "piston of the Intifada".[62] Its main impulse was to smash the system that systematically violated the dignity of individuals and people.[63]

One of the main tangible "proofs" for this characterization seems to be the fact that most of the rioters arrested on the first day had no previous record nor were known as active in any Palestinian movement. This youth appeared to be ignorant of political affairs. Hardly any of the detainees knew the clauses of the Palestinian National Convent nor the slogans used in PLO-propaganda. In the interrogations it turned out that the rebels were mainly labourers working in Israel. Many gave the same motive for their participation in the riots. They were protesting against the personal injustice inflicted upon them by their Jewish employers and colleagues, the humiliation suffered repeatedly at roadblocks and checkpoints. These experiences made many detainees believe that the Israelis were capable of almost anything.[64]

The disciplined boycotts drastically curtailed the trade between the Territories and Israel. This led to a change in the pattern of consumption ending the excessive consumerism of recent years which had only served the Israeli and Jordanian economy and prevented the accumulation of capital so desperately needed for the Palestinian economy.[65] It seems as if many Palestinians became aware of the need to adopt consumption patters more in accordance with their economic and national interests. The economy of the Territories became reduced to an economy of subsistence, bringing different strata of society close together. The need for solidarity under the Occupation was felt more strongly than ever before.

The main characteristic of the *Intifāḍa* was its popular nature. It was based on a network established at the grass-roots integrating the mass of the Palestinian population. "Popular committees" sprang up in almost every city.[66] Even though some observers thought that the mass-based uprising had occurred spontaneously, it has to be seen in the context of a long sustained history of mass organisation among the Palestinians. The *Intifāḍa* could more exactly be described as the result and climax of accumulated historical experience.

The emergence of popular mass organisations in the Occupied Territories can be traced to the mid 1970's.[67] This was the starting point for the assertion of a distinctive identity of the Occupied Territories within the Palestinian world community. This was due to the need to find a more appropriate form of action under the oppressive Israeli rule which tried to destroy any Palestinian organisation by means of detention and expulsion of its leaders. In the period from 1972 to 1975 the Palestinians realized that the occupation was not going to be of short duration. Thus rudiments of a national infrastructure were laid down. Newspapers and voluntary work movements, such as the Union of Palestinian Medical Relief Committees, were founded and the universities opened their doors for all strata of society.[68] Since 1976 the formal entry of segments of the underprivileged strata of the society, such as wage labourers, into institutional Palestinian life can be observed. Youth, women, labourers and other specific groups of Palestinian society were mobilized under slogans of social progress and national independence. This is in a sharp contrast to earlier stages of the national struggle when the national movement remained relatively isolated from society and lacked a mass base despite its general legitimacy.[69] The characteristic of the mass movements was less their material infrastructure which could easily be blocked by the Israelis, than voluntary work done by the people.[70] By building up alternative self-help-organisations, the status quo was defied and the framework for the national question broadened. "The new perspective thus combined both national and social elements".[71]

According to these social and political transformations, the cultural activities of the Palestinians put greater emphasis on informal, collective aspects for reinforcing the spirit of cohesion and unity. Here, commitment to the national cause and assertion of national identity have become the basic components and goals of cultural activities and the acid test of their "relevance". Parallel to the evolution on a political and social level, the Israeli closure of academic and cultural institutions serving Palestinian self-expression contributed directly to this popularization of cultural life. "The *Intifāḍa*'s political, social and economic disengagement from Israeli occupation as a negation of its authority is expressed in the emergence of an essentially engaged Palestinian culture which draws upon its own authentic resources and frames of reference".[72]

The leaders of the popular uprising – united more or less in the Unified National Command with the exception of *Ḥamās* – differed from the traditional Palestinian leadership which was mainly an urban, middle class elite.[73] It was the famous *shabāb* (youth) that grew up under occupation and lost faith in diplomacy and intercession with the authorities. The United National Command challenged the infallibility of the PLO-leaders regarded as bureaucrats living far from the "theatre of operations".[74]

I want the reader to bear in mind the feeling of a need for and display of solidarity, the overwhelming suspicion and hatred towards the Israelis, the poor economic situation, the mass-based institutional and political life, as well as the strong cultural assertion predominant in Palestinian society under occupation. Islamic ideology as expounded by the Islamic Resistance Movement was initially developed in this environment.

NOTES

1. Wilfred Cantwell Smith in his very sensitive work *Islam in Modern History*, (Princeton, 1957), insists at length on this point. See especially pp. 95ff, 113ff.
2. Smith describes the defensive interpretation as "the most serious intellectual development within the religion in recent times". Ibid, p. 121.
3. Montgomery Watt, *Islamic Fundamentalism and Modernity*, (London, 1988), p. 51.
4. Zubaida, "The Quest for the Islamic State", p. 44.
5. Rudolph Peters, "Erneuerungsbewegungen im Islam vom 18. bis 20. Jahrhundert und die Rolle des Islams in der neueren Geschichte: Antikolonialismus und Nationalismus", p. 125. In: Werner Ende/Udo Steinbach (eds), *Der Islam in der Gegenwart*, (München, 1984), pp. 91–132.

6. Montgomery Watt, *Islamic Political Thought. The Basic Concepts*, (Edinburgh, 1968), pp. 52–53.
7. As we will see in later chapters of this volume, contemporary fundamentalists absorb many Western concepts and ideas despite proclamations of their total refusal to do so.
8. Peters, "Erneuerungsbewegungen im Islam vom 18. bis 20. Jahrhundert und die Rolle des Islams in der neueren Geschichte: Antikolonialismus und Nationalismus", p. 127
9. Zubaida, "The Quest for the Islamic State", p. 47.
10. Hasan al-Banna strongly objected to political parties, which he saw as threatening the unity of the *Umma*. See the standard reference work on the Muslim Brotherhood, Richard P. Mitchell, *The Society of the Muslim Brothers*, (London, 1969), pp. 218–220.
11. This strategy made the Muslim Brotherhood one of the few parties that did not rely strongly on patronage and clientelism for its support. See Zubaida, "The Quest for an Islamic State", p. 50.
12. The secret apparatus' most famous victim was the Egyptian Prime Minister, al-Nuqrashi, who was shot in 1949.
13. See Saad Eddin Ibrahim, "An Islamic Alternative in Egypt: The Muslim Brotherhood and Sadat". In: *Arab Studies Quarterly*, Vol. 4, No. 1 & 2, 1982, pp. 75–93.
14. In Egypt the groups "Repentance and Holy Flight" (*al-takfīr wa-l-hijra*) and the "Islamic Liberation Organisation" (known as *al-fanniyya al-'askariyya* since its take over of the Technical Military Academy). On these groups see Saad Eddin Ibrahim, "Anatomy of Egypt's Militant Islamic Groups: Methodological Note and Preliminary Findings". In: *International Journal for Middle East Studies*, 12, 1980, pp. 423–453.
15. See Johannes Reissner, "Die militant-islamischen Gruppen", p. 473. In: Ende/Steinbach, *Der Islam in der Gegenwart*, pp. 470–487.
16. Published for the first time in Cairo in 1949. I will hithero use the 4th edition, (Cairo,1954), p. 19.
17. Ibid, pp. 16–17.
18. Kepel, *Le Prophète et le Pharaon. Les Movements Islamiques dans l'Egypte Contemporaine*, p. 45.
19. He summarized his main ideas in his late work *Ma'ālim fi-l-Ṭarīq*, (Cairo, 1964), which can be considered as an instruction for bringing about the Islamic Order.
20. See his commentary of the Sura "The Table" (5). In: *Fī Ẓilāl al-Qur'ān*, p. 891.
21. Ibid.
22. Muhammad Qutb in the Introduction to the English translation of his brother's Tafsīr *In the Shade of the Qur'ān*, (London, 1979), p. xvi.
23. Ibid, p. xi.
24. Ibid, p. xiii.
25. Youssef M.Choueiri, *Islamic Fundamentalism* (London, 1990), pp. 110ff.
26. Ibid, p. 90; Kepel, *Le Prophète et le Pharaon. Les Movements Islamiques dans l'Egypte Contemporaine*, p. 50.

27. *Tafhīm al-Qur'ān*, six volumes, published 1950–1973. See English translation (*Towards Understanding the Qur'an*, Leicester, 1988) of volume I, Foreword, p. xiii.
28. Fouad Ajami, *The Arab Predicament. Arab Political Thought and Practice Since 1967*, (Cambridge, 1981), p. 8.
29. Ibid, p. 40.
30. Ajami sees "self" and "authenticity" as the Arab-Muslim substitutes for the European "liberty" and "equality". Ibid, p. 171.
31. Ibid, p. 73.
32. See Milton-Edwards, *Islamic Politics in Palestine*, (London, 1996) for a detailed account and analysis of the development of the Palestinian Islamic movements since 1935.
33. *Ḥamās* claims to have started the *Intifāḍa* and to have issued its first *Bayān* (leaflet) the 15 December 1987. See FM, January 1990, p. 21. Schiff and Ya'ari describe the Muslim Brotherhood overtaken by the militant mood in the streets. Only in February 1988 Sheikh Yassin founded the new militant branch *Ḥamās*. Schiff, Ze'ev, Ya'ari, Ehud, *Intifada: The Palestinian Uprising, Israel's Third Front*, (New York, 1990), pp. 222 and 224.
34. David McDowall, "A Profile of the Population of the West Bank and Gaza Strip", p. 20. In: *Journal of Refugee Studies*, 2(1), (1989), pp. 20–26.
35. Sarah Roy,"The Gaza Strip: Critical Effects of the Occupation", p. 249. In: Naseer Aruri (ed), *Occupation. Israel over Palestine*, 2nd ed, (Belmont, 1989), pp. 249–297.
36. McDowall, op. cit., pp. 20–21. These estimations are based on the Central Bureau of Statistic's report *Projections of Population in Judea, Samaria and the Gaza Area up to 2002*, (Jerusalem, 1987).
37. Schiff/Ya'ari, op. cit., p. 89.
38. Naseer Aruri, "Dialectics of Dispossession", p. 16. In: Aruri (ed), *Occupation. Israel over Palestine.*, pp. 1–48.
39. McDowall, op. cit., p. 23.
40. Sarah Roy, "The Gaza Strip: Critical Effects of the Occupation", pp. 295–296. This evaluation does not contradict the fact that from one perspective Israel's occupation has introduced limited economic prosperity resulting from the creation of wage labour inside Israel that is better paid than inside the Territories. (This is in fact one of the Israeli arguments to justify the occupation.) But most of this money went directly back into the Israeli economy through the purchase of consumer goods.
41. See Sarah Graham-Brown, "The Economic Consequences of the Occupation", in: Aruri, *Occupation. Israel over Palestine*, pp. 297–360. Schiff and Ya'ari describe the Territories as being hold hostage to the Israeli economy, op. cit., p. 91.
42. Taraki, "Mass Organisations in the West Bank", p. 439. In 1970 around 12.8 percent of the labour force of the West Bank was employed in Israel, in 1980 it were 30 percent. In the Gaza Strip the increase was from 10 percent in 1970 to about 43 percent in 1980. Graham-Brown, "The Economic Consequences of the Occupation", p. 341.

43. Benvenisti, Meron, *The West Bank Data Project. Demographic, Legal, Social and Political Developments in the West Bank, Report 1987* (Boulder, 1987), p. 52.
44. Graham-Brown,"The Economic Consequences of the Occupation", p. 309.
45. Adam Roberts, "The Palestinians, the Uprising, and International Law", p. 33. In: *Journal for Refugee Studies*, 2(1), 1989, pp. 26–40.
46. Ibid.
47. Ibid, p. 345.
48. Ziad Abu-Amr, "Class Structure and the Political Elite in the Gaza Strip: 1948–1988", p. 86. In: Aruri (ed), *Occupation. Israel over Palestine*, pp. 77–98.
49. This is mainly true for the Gaza Strip. See Abu-Amr, "Class Structure and the Political Elite in the Gaza Strip", pp. 78–80.
50. Graham-Brown, "The Economic Consequences of the Occupation", p. 320.
51. Ibid, p. 321.
52. Ibid.
53. Munir Fasheh, "Education under Occupation", p. 513. In: Aruri, *Occupation. Israel over Palestine*, pp. 511–535.
54. Graham-Brown, "The Economic Consequences of the Occupation", p. 351.
55. Sarah Graham-Brown, "Impact on the Social Structure of Palestinian Society", p. 380. In: Aruri, *Occupation. Israel over Palestine*, pp. 361–397.
56. Fasheh, op. cit., p. 530.
57. Ibid.
58. In 1981 more than 1000 titles were banned from the libraries in the Territories. In 1967 an Israeli military order banned 78 out of 121 textbooks that had officially been approved by the Jordanian Ministry of Education. Ibid, pp. 518 and 516.
59. Fasheh, op. cit., p. 513.
60. Friedhelm Ernst, "Problems of UNRWA School education and Vocational Training", p. 91. In: *Journal of Refugee Studies*, 2(1),1989, pp. 88–98.
61. Schiff/Ya'ari, op. cit., p. 79.
62. Ibid, p. 93.
63. Ibid, p. 80.
64. Ibid, p. 83. Most of the less educated believed that the traffic accident of December 8th had been a deliberate act of vengeance of the Israelis. Ibid.
65. Hisham Awartani, "Obstacles to Opportunity", p. 68. In: *Journal of Refugee Studies*, 2(1),1989, pp. 64–70.
66. Schiff/Ya'ari, op. cit., p.188.
67. Lisa Taraki, "Mass Organisations in the West Bank", p. 432.
68. Ibid, p. 440.
69. Ibid, p. 434.
70. Barghouti, op. cit., p. 126.
71. Ibid, p. 128.

72. Hanan Mikhail Ashrawi, "The Politics of Cultural Revival", pp. 78–79. In: Michael C. Hudson (ed), *The Palestinians: New Directions* (Washington, 1990), p. 82.
73. Abed, op. cit., p. 56; Abu Amr,"The Politics of the Intifada", p. 11. In: Hudson (ed), *The Palestinians: New Directions*, pp. 3–24.
74. Ibid, p. 189. Schiff and Ya'ari report the fierce struggle of the PLO against any "sub-command" in the Territories by presenting the Unified Leadership as the "arm" of the PLO. Finally the United Leadership "swallowed its resentment over the rigid guardianship of the PLO". Op. cit., p. 192.

PART ONE

The Basic Themes in the Thought of *Ḥamās*

CHAPTER TWO

The Problem: Israel, Zionism and the Jews

The main problem for the Muslims to resolve is the existence of the Jewish state of Israel in the middle of the Arab-Muslim world. It constitutes a constant reminder of the weakness and deep crisis of the Islamic *Umma* that does not have the strength to get rid of this "cancer" (*saraṭān*)[1]. The Jewish state is presented by *Ḥamās* as a purely religious state which is part of a world-wide Jewish conspiracy against the Muslims in particular and the whole world in general. On these grounds, all Muslims have the duty to fight the Jewish enemy. The existence of Israel is called by the Qur'ānic term of *bāṭil*, the liberation of Palestine and the establishment of an Islamic Palestinian state is viewed as *ḥaqq*.[2] The dichotomous character of the world-view advanced by the Qur'ān is thus applied to the conflict with Israel. But – paradoxically or as a consequence – the fact that Israel is perceived to be based on religious laws, and the efficiency of world Jewry in achieving its religious interests at the same time, inspires profound admiration and serves as a model for a coming Islamic Palestinian state.

The vocabulary used to describe the Jews is highly indicative of the Qur'ānic and Western sources from which it is derived. Qur'ānic vocabulary and paraphrases are often blended with pejorative expressions from certain modern Christian anti-Semitic writings rather than from classical Islamic ones. In the Qur'ān, *Ḥadīth*, *Tafsīr* and other theoretical literature, the Jews are named as "*Banū Isrā'īl*" and "*al-Yahūd*", or the names of the Jewish tribes of Medina are mentioned. The Palestinian Islamists use the term "*al-Yahūd*" as well as "unbelievers" (*kāfirūn*).[3] They also use characterisations of the Jews as "the people upon whom God's anger came" which can be found in many places in the Qur'ān as well as in the *Sūrat al-Fātiḥa*[4] and which are generally interpreted as designating the Jews. The Qur'ānic terms *bāṭil* and *ḥaqq* are used to designate the two parties involved in the conflict.

The Jews are said not to "spare any effort to develop plans and plots to destroy human life since God's anger came upon them".[5] God's anger came upon them because they did not follow properly the religion he sent them, but they killed his prophets and distorted the originally Godly Jewish religion.[6] Most especially, they tried to harm the Islamic *Umma* and to dominate it because it is the "new international force bringing an authentic civilisatory and godly programme to mankind".[7]

These are basic Qur'ānic ideas. God had sent his message to mankind first to the Jews in form of the Torah,[8] but they turned away[9] and did not believe his signs and falsified them.[10] When they did not like the message of a Prophet, they called him a liar and killed him.[11] After God had sent them the Prophet Moses, they set up the Golden Calf as their God.[12] That is why "they were burdened with wrath from God."[13] As the Jews had strayed from the right path God had to send another Prophet, Muhammad. His message, Islam, is merely a repetition and completion of the Godly message that had been sent to the Jews and Christians before.[14] Thus every true believer among the Jews and Christians must recognise the new Prophet and his message.[15] But as the new Prophet was chosen among the Arabs and thus ended the leading role of Jews and Christians, they showed hostility towards the new Prophet out of envy.[16]

There is no doubt that for the Islamists the "Zionist entity" (*al-kiyān al-ṣahyūnī*) – the name "Israel" is used only exceptionally to describe the Jewish state – was founded as a religious state.[17] Religious beliefs based on the Torah shape Zionist thought and determine life in Israel until today.[18] The Islamists find proof of this "fundamental truth"[19] in the slightest detail. The name of the state, "Israel", is of a religious nature, just as "Knesset" or "Histadrud". More importantly the education of young Israelis is based on the religious creed. Starting at the age of five children are sent to Kibbutzim to get physical and spiritual education according to the Torah,[20] in secondary school, four hours a week are consecrated to Torah-studies, one hour to the study of the Talmud. The Hebrew language was revived after it had been dead for 2000 years, and all new immigrants get new Jewish names at their arrival. The Israeli army uses military tactics taught by the Torah, such as expulsion, destruction of houses and the policy of scorched earth. Food also has to conform to religious rules, and religious institutions supervise all restaurants in Israel. Thus Begin on his visit to Cairo had kosher food flown in every day for him and his entourage. The sabbath-rules are observed throughout the country and Begin issued a law banning flights of the national airline "El Al" on Saturdays. When Begin travelled to Cairo for Sadat's funeral, he lived in a tent near Medinat Nasser in order to be able to walk to the ceremony which was held on a Saturday. Never has an Israeli military strike started on a Saturday. All these details prove how meticulously the Jews respect their religious laws.

At this point, the ambiguous attitude of the Islamists towards the "Zionist entity" clearly appears. Intended as a portrayal of the religious character of the battle against the Jewish state, this alleged strict observance by Israelis of the Jewish religious rules clearly shows the Islamists' admiration and is taken as an example of how Muslims should behave. It is interesting to note that the Jews of Israel are presented as people truly following their religious laws and customs and thereby attaining success. In sections on the Israeli state *Filasṭīn al-Muslima* rarely mentions the classical Qur'ānic view of the Jews as straying from the right godly path and as having distorted and falsified their religion. (It is nonetheless presented in other sections of the journal, as I have already shown). The Islamists seem to exclude voluntarily these aspects of the Qur'ānic teaching in order to convince their own people that only a return to the Islamic religion guarantees success. The mobilising character of the writing overrides theoretical subtleties.

The example of the Jewish state gives detailed indications of how an Islamic Palestinian state should be organised. Israel has no written constitution, but the Ministry of Religious Affairs controls every law issued by the Knesset to ensure its accordance with the Torah.[21] If the state is sometimes too slow or unwilling to implement religious laws and to supervise their observance, truly religious people (*al-qubba'āt al-sūd* or black hats)[22] themselves go into the street and control their fellow citizens.[23]

However the strength of the "Zionist enemy" is not only based on the people's respect for its religious laws, it also lies in its mastery of the modern world and its technological inventions. Thus Israel has for a long time acknowledged the importance of television, the "most dangerous contemporary medium that shapes the mind of individuals".[24] Israel's skillful use of this influential instrument has provided it with the support of the Western people for her "falsehood" (*bāṭil*).[25] The Islamic media are criticised as still being incapable of success.[26] The Libyan Ahmed Abd al-Rahman is praised for forming a communication society, and producing films, conferences and discussions in Great Britain. More such initiatives are needed to present the Islamic point of view.[27]

The "Zionist entity" also succeeded in exploiting to its own advantage the transformation of the world after the break-down of Eastern Europe.[28] On the Arab side there was no real effort to influence the series of changes.[29] Another example of "Jewish success" is detected in the question of German reunification which gave rise to great fears among the Jews. They demanded from East-Germany the recognition of Israel and an apology for the slaughter of Jews under Nazi-rule – and got both.[30]

The Islamists are aware that the perceived upholding of religious laws is not the only reason for the success of the "Zionist entity". International Jewry's defence of Israel's interests in the world is the other main feature of the enemy. Jews are seen to hold important positions all over the world which they use to promote the Zionist cause. According to the Islamists, many Jewish professors are working in Western academic institutions in order to dominate them.[31] The same is true for the world of the media, which explains why foreign books and newspapers are "generally subservient to the Jewish position".[32] The world's armies are similarly seen as being infiltrated by Jews, and the presence of the US-army on the Holy Saudi-Arabian soil is therefore all the more dangerous.[33] The intimate link between Israel and the Jewish communities in the Diaspora was highlighted by the government crisis of 1990 when Menahem Shneerson, the head of the Lubavich movement in New York, advised the members of the religious parties in the Knesset on whom they should allow to form a government. A religious Jew, who had never visited Israel, is determining the politics of the

"Zionist entity" from his house in New York![34] Historically, the Jews are discerned behind "most of the world revolutions such as the French and the Russian one. They are seen as the manipulators of the First and Second (!) World War.[35] They founded organisations like the Rotary or the Lion's Club whose purpose is seen as espionage and whose money rules the imperialist world.[36]

In the traditional theoretical literature there is clearly a basis for an accusation of espionage and plotting against the Muslims. In the Qur'ān, the Jews are presented as having turned their backs on God's signs and as having "disobeyed and transgressed"; they "corrupt (...) on earth."[37] Mawdūdī points out that the Qur'ān informs the Muslims of the "machinations of the Jews against Islam and the Muslims", of the Jews' efforts to contaminate the "simple and pure-hearted Muslims with the spiritual diseases from which they themselves suffered".[38] They are committing acts of "treachery"[39] and the Muslims are warned not to take Jews or Christians as friends because they are friends with each other (but not with the Muslims).[40] "As often as they kindle a fire for war, God will extinguish it. They seek corruption in the land (...)."[41] Early biographical and *Ḥadīth* literature contains even more examples of how the Jews tried to harm the Muslim community and its leader. Once they try to kill Muhammad with a rock thrown from the top of a house;[42] then they come to spy out weaknesses.[43] The Jewish Rabbis strove to introduce confusion among the Muslims by pretending to be converted to Islam, without having done so "in their hearts".[44] Only individual Jews are said to have accepted Islam and thus proven their true belief in God.[45] But in the end, Muslims do not need to fear the Jews because they are cowards who "will not fight against you as one body except in fortified towns or from behind walls".[46] The Jews do not have the strength and worldly power to realize their plots. All these allegations against the Jews of falsehood, envy, treachery, mischief and cowardice are put forward in the framework of the struggle of Jewish tribes against the Muslim community in Medina and the misbehaviour of the *Banū Isrā'īl*.

The evolution of the accounts of this struggle into an international conspiracy-theory was only possible in the 20th century with its global interconnections and world-wide communication. Still this does not explain the major departure from the traditional Islamic stereotype of the Jews. The Jews are no longer cowards who will always be humiliated and kept in place by the Muslims. This image of wretchedness and humiliation associated with the Jews in the traditional Islamic image, which was sustained by the strength and confidence of Islamic civilisation until at least the 15th century,[47] is now superseded by that of the powerful Jew, seriously threatening the Muslim community and the whole world. Furthermore, a set of terms is used which are different from the traditional Islamic ones. The Jews are described as "Jewish satan"[48], the "bloodsucker of mankind"[49], "racists", "criminals of the tribe of Zion"[50] and "Nazis".[51] The Islamists justify the doubtful historical analogy and the use of the notion "Jewish Nazism" by characterising the crime of a people's expulsion from their homeland as "a kind of murder".[52]

In this transformation of the image of the Jew, we can clearly detect traces of modern European anti-Semitism. This influence is particularly obvious in the wide circulation of the "Protocols of the Elders of Zion" in the Arab world. These forged anti-Semitic documents, which circulated in Europe in the 1920s and 1930s, were translated into Arabic for the first time in 1926.[53] They are quoted in the *Mīthāq* of *Ḥamās* as a proof for the allegations against the Jews.[54] The "Protocols" are supposed to prove the existence of a "Jewish government which, through a world-wide network of camouflaged agencies and organisations, controls political parties and governments, the press and public opinion, banks and economic development".[55] This "report" of a member of the secret Jewish government – the Elders of Zion – is the most influential in a long series of anti-Semitic forgeries reaching back almost to the French Revolution.[56] It represents the peak of the myth of a Jewish world-conspiracy which Cohn defines as a "modern adaptation" of an "ancient demonological tradition" going back to the second century when Christianity and Judaism competed for converts in the Hellenistic world.[57] Norman Cohn's characterisation of these texts as a blending of remnants of ancient demonological terrors with anxieties and resentments which are typically modern[58] is particularly interesting in our context, as modern Islamist thought can be described in similar terms.

This Islamisation of Western anti-Semitic ideas is in no way unique to the Palestinian fundamentalists.[59] One of the most widespread contemporary books on the question, *The Jews in the Qur'ān* by

'Afif 'Abd al-Fattah Tabbara – the eleventh edition was printed in 1986[60] – follows these lines. Qur'ānic verses are not only interpreted in the light of *Ḥadīths* about the various Jewish conspiracies against Mohammad and his followers, such as the refusal to pay back debts after the creditor converted to Islam,[61] the spread of doubts among the Muslims,[62] and formal conversion without conviction in order to trouble Muslims.[63] Furthermore, long passages from Adolf Hitler's *Mein Kampf* are quoted,[64] apparently to give the often very general and abstract Qur'ānic verses a more concrete meaning. The Qur'ānic characterisations of the *Banū Isrā'īl* as liars and ungrateful trouble-makers are thus confirmed to be eternal and unchanging and these attributes also apply to the Jews living in Israel today. This conviction represents a variation of the idea of the unchangingness of human nature which is a characteristic trait of the traditional Islamic world-view.[65] Thus, without any further reflection, the link to the present struggle in Palestine can be made: "What the Qur'ān says [about the Jews] can be perfectly applied to the Jewish Zionists today".[66]

In fact, Christian anti-Semitism had penetrated the Arab world in the 19th century and was originally spread by Christian Arab minorities.[67] In the middle of the century, the first Arabic versions of European writings appeared. The penetration of anti-Semitism in its European Christian form was slow and only became a major factor in the Arab world in the later 1950s and 1960s.[68] It evolved in direct connection to the developments in Palestine. The foundation of the Jewish state in 1948 and the succession of Arab-Muslim military defeats against the Jewish army came as a shock and posed a serious psychological problem: how could the weak and cowardly Jews inflict humiliation on the Muslims? These developments appeared to be incompatible with the traditional view of the Jews. In the search for an explanation, European anti-Semitism was welcomed. By demonising the Jews and presenting them as the sons of Satan engaged in a conspiracy against all mankind, they became a truly strong adversary. At the same time this procedure gives a "cosmic stature"[69] to those who fight them and secures their dignity – even in defeat. Accordingly, the Palestinian Islamists consider the war between the Jewish state and the Palestinian people not merely as a struggle between these two groups, but see the Zionists as "part of the international Jewishhood" and part of the Western alliance.[70] The

Palestinians, on the other hand, are part of the Islamic *Umma* and the *Dār al-Islām*.

One of the most important changes to have occurred under the impact of Israel's superiority and the growing Arab anti-Semitism resulting from it, is a new emphasis in Islamic writing on the Jews. Even though the Qur'ān and the theoretical Islamic literature devote much attention to the *Banū Isrā'il* and to the Jewish tribes of Medina, they only represent a minor, localised nuisance.[71] Muslim theologians and polemicists of the past devoted little theoretical and practical attention to Judaism which they perceived as of "minor importance and offering no serious challenge".[72] For centuries, the main political enemy of Islam was Christianity. In contrast, Islamic thought in the 20th century has become obsessed with the issue of Zionism.[73] Voluminous literature on the Jews and their misdeeds was produced as the Jews became central to the consciousness of Muslims.[74] Anti-Jewish teaching was transformed into a comprehensive living philosophy and the Jew became a general metaphor for danger and threat to Islam.[75]

It is important to stress that Islamic anti-Semitism is fundamentally different from its Western Christian predecessor. It is the result of a political conflict over territory, of a clash over real interests.[76] Arab resentments against Jews are not at the origin of the conflict. This Islamic anti-Semitism was developed as a weapon in the struggle against Israel, whose existence is the starting point of the whole conflict. One major component of modern Western-style anti-Semitism is lacking in the Arab-Islamic version: racism. The evil image of the Jews is based on their religion and their spiritual character, but not on their race or blood. Thus Islamic anti-Semitism can be described as "superficial"[77] compared with its Western Christian counterpart, but directed against a real enemy and threat.

Curiously, the fact that the Islamists have a concrete enemy to confront did not prevent the disappearance of the distinction between Israelis, Zionists and Jews. They use these terms alternately and synonymously in their texts. Nevertheless, the Islamists claim to distinguish between "Zionism" and "Judaism": Judaism is considered a "religion that stipulates racism and hostility towards others in its books and incites to wrongly take away Palestine under the slogan of the Holy Land".[78] Zionism "represents the entity of the enemy" (Israel) and is "responsible for the transformation of Jewish thought into a reality that is perceptible today in Palestine".[79] Zionists are those Jews who want to realise their religious thought on Muslim soil.[80] Basically, all Jews outside Palestine are considered non-Zionists if they do not actively support the "Zionist entity".[81] Jews inside Palestine are considered as Zionists if they do not prove that they oppose the Jewish occupation of any part of Palestinian soil.[82] Referring to Israel, the Islamists mainly use the notion of "Zionist entity", probably in order to avoid using the term "Israel" which may be considered an implicit recognition of the state. The negative connotations of Zionism have furthermore been legitimised internationally when the United Nations General Assembly passed a resolution that included Zionism among racist ideologies.[83] Otherwise, the Israelis are mainly referred to as "the Jews" which establishes the link to the sayings of the Qur'ān and the *Ḥadīth* about the Jews. As Joseph Nevo suggests, it is easier to focus one's hostility on a familiar target, the Jews, rather than on an abstract and vague Zionist demon.[84]

The Islamists claim to confine their interpretation to the realm of Islamic *fiqh* which respects Jews and Christians as *ahl al-kitāb*. Jews and Christians are called "the people of the Book" by Muslims as opposed to "heathens" because they recognize the divine books, Torah and Gospel, even though they transmitted them in a falsified form. After their submission to Islam as a ruling force they were granted free worship and protection in return for payment of a poll-tax. Violation of this defence-alliance by Muslims is considered a perfidy.[85] The Islamic order is considered by the fundamentalists as the most just and humane organisation of society and its religious groups. *Ḥamās* states that it does not take action against anybody because of his thought or religious convictions, as long as these are not transformed into perceptible hostility towards and destruction of the rights of the Islamic *Umma*.[86] But this is exactly the case in Palestine. The Jews in Palestine are aggressors that occupy Muslim land and are therefore considered "war enemies".[87] Muslims are no longer bound by the Islamic teaching that demands respect for the defence-alliance with *ahl al-kitāb*. The Jews are fought because of the hostile action they take against Muslims.[88] The Islamists thus make sure that their struggle is perceived as conforming to the traditional Islamic teaching that nobody can be persecuted because of his beliefs. Fighting against non-Muslims in order to convert them by force to the Muslim creed is outlawed.[89]

Furthermore, the Israeli Jews' racism (*'unṣūriyya*) has to be fought. Their treatment of Oriental Jews, as well as their Arab citizens, who are relegated to the ranks of second class citizens, proves their racism.[90] But *Ḥamās* also struggles on behalf of the Christians, who are equally oppressed by the Zionists.[91] The racist nature of the "Zionist entity" is underlined by regular reports about Israel's close ties with South Africa, whose regime was internationally marked as racist.[92] This accusation has been very common in the Arab world and in secular national Arabic thought since the late 1960s.[93] This definition is vaguely rooted in the traditional Islamic characterisation of the Jews as arrogant and selfish, a view based on the Jewish notion of the "chosen people", but it seems just as likely that today all evil qualities are somehow ascribed to the Jews.

The evil of Zionism has to be eradicated at its root. The Islamists do this by "proving" that all historical claims to the land of Palestine by the Zionists are false. First of all, they are not direct descendants of the tribe of *Banū Isrā'īl* who once lived in Palestine.[94] According to a theory advanced in the beginning of this century the European Jews are not of Israelite descendance, but the offspring of a tribe of Central Asian Turks converted to Judaism, called *Khazzār*. The fact that the Qur'ānic characterisations of the *Banū Isrā'īl*, and guidelines about interaction with them are at the same time directly related to Israel and its population does not seem to strike the Islamists as contradictory. In a series entitled "The Qur'ānic truth about the Palestine question", it is shown that the Qur'ān refutes any historical claim of the "Israeli Jews" on Palestine. The Jewish religious and cultural heritage is simply presented as part of Islamic "history" and thus subordinated to it. This assertion is derived from the fact that God only revealed one and the same message several times to mankind, first in the form of the Torah, later in the form of the Gospels and finally in the form of Islam. History in Islamic terms is not a sequence of events, but the expression of a faith in a system of life and a community.[95] *Ḥamās* "reads in history" that the Islamic rule established over Palestine under the *Khulafā' Rāshida* (the rightly guided caliphs) is a mere extension of the "Islamic rule" of David and Solomon who reigned according to God's programme.[96] They were in fact Islamic kings. This springs directly from the conviction that every "true" believer is automatically a Muslim. Abraham is accordingly considered the first "true Muslim", as the "father of the prophets" as well as the "father of the Muslims."[97] We can read in the biographical literature as well as in the Qur'ān that "Abraham was neither a Jew nor a Christian but he was a Muslim *ḥanīf* (...)."[98] Thus the Jews cannot refer to an ancestral line to Abraham who built the first mosque on earth, the Ka'ba, as claimed in the Qur'ān and the *Ḥadīth*.[99] Al-Aqṣā is, according to a *Ḥadīth*, the second mosque built on earth forty years after the Ka'ba, and was also built by Abraham.[100] Thus the Islamic presence in Palestine has a longer history than the Jewish one and all Israeli claims that Solomon had first built a temple on the site of the present Al-Aqṣā mosque are lies. "Isn't it a historical fact that Abraham lived a hundred years before Solomon?"[101] So the historical argument which Jews invoke to defend their right to live in Palestine in fact works against them.[102]

The Islamists have no problem integrating the other historical fact that says that when the Muslims conquered Palestine there was no Al-Aqṣā mosque in Jerusalem. The historical evidence indicates that the Dome of the Rock was built in the years 69–72 by 'Abd al-Malik. Islamists have no doubt that Abraham built the mosque and then "God alone knows what happened and who, when and why destroyed it". It was then "rebuilt" after the Muslims entered Jerusalem.[103] "We do not see any contradiction between the Qur'ānic report and the historical reality".[104]

This procedure to "Islamise" all of history before Muhammad – which comes from the basic Qur'ānic teaching that only one godly message was sent to earth – is worth examining more closely. It recognises the achievements of the past and of other peoples without the need to pay tribute to them. This allows the integration of all kinds of "alien" ideas and achievements without the acknowledgment of their foreign origin. This mind-set, going back to the Qur'ān and the earliest days of Islam, strikes me as basic for understanding modern Islamic movements of an apologetic and also fundamentalist nature. As I will show later, this procedure is applied by modern fundamentalists, allowing them to present even Western concepts like democracy and nationalism as Islamic principles.

As the Jews have no historical right to Palestine, Israel is an "artificial" state.[105] The best proof of this is the fact that Israel always needed workmen from outside its territory, as it could not provide enough within its own borders.[106] The Jewish state was the creation of "world-Imperialism under the guidance of the US"[107] and could only survive as a "military state swarming with soldiers".[108] Its existence depends at all levels on the support from the Jewish "*bourgeoisie*"[109] outside the country. "The Jews think that they found a solution to their problem but in fact they created a new problem for the Palestinian people".[110] The Jewish problem will not be resolved until the Palestinians get back their land.[111]

The link between the "Zionist entity" and the "international Jewish conspiracy" finds its most recent expression in the mass immigration of Soviet Jews to Palestine.[112] This population influx forced Israel to expand its borders and thus was seen to bring the Zionists one step closer to their dream of a "Great Israel".[113] For the Islamists there is no doubt that the goal of the Zionist project is to "widen the physical boundaries" of the existing entity[114] in order to dominate the whole region.[115] In the *Mīthāq* the Zionist plans are in a general way described as being without limits, aiming at an extension of their rule "from the Nile to the Euphrates".[116] As a proof for this allegation, the Islamists mention the conspiratory plans described in the "Protocols of the Elder of Zion".[117] In the magazine *Filasṭīn al-Muslima*, the accusations become more concrete. The Zionists want to swallow Jordan at the first opportunity,[118] but they will not stop their expansion once they take over Jordan – something the leaders of the other Arab countries do not want to see nor face. Israel's invasions of Lebanon as well as the Israeli-Ethiopian cooperation, which served to build up a security belt around the Red Sea, demonstrated clearly its genuine expansionist nature.[119] For this reason peace proposals will only "widen the appetite" of the Zionists,[120] who try to win time by any means in order to better establish their state.[121]

The argument that Zionism is of an intrinsically expansionist nature was at times also common in secular Arab nationalism.[122] The name of "Eretz Israel" used by certain Jews to claim biblical borders for Israel is a proof for this allegation as well as the steady expansion of the Jewish settlements in Palestine.[123] Y. Harkabi speculates that the idea of

Zionist expansion was emphasised in Arab ideology in order to justify the "extreme nature of the objective", the destruction of the state of Israel.[124]

NOTES

1. This expression is very common to denote "Israel" not only in fundamentalist literature, but in nationalist Arab writing. See Y. Harkabi, *Arab Attitudes to Israel*, (London, 1972), p. 70.
2. *Mīthāq*. p. 12. These antipodes of God's "truth" and the unbeliever's "falsehood" are at the very basis of the Qur'ānic world-view. They contain the core of the Islamic programme: "to make firm the true (*ḥaqq*) and to annul the untrue (*bāṭil*), even though the perfidious might be averse." Qur'ān, 8.8.
3. FM, January 1990, p. 52.
4. In the common interpretation of the *Sūrat al-Fātiḥa* it is the Jews who are seen in the last lines ("not those upon whom wrath falls, nor those who are perverse") – even though this was probably not the original intention. See Harkabi, op. cit., p. 221.
5. FM, November 1990, p. 7.
6. FM, April 1990, p. 25.
7. Ibid, p. 24.
8. Qur'ān, 2:47: "O children of Israel, remember My favours which I have bestowed upon you, and that I preferred you to all beings."
9. Ibid, 9:76: "But when He conferred upon them His bounty they were avaricious with it; and they turned away, swerving aside."
10. Ibid, 2:61: "(...)That was because they disbelieved in God's signs...". Ibid, 2:75: "Are you eager that they should believe in you when a party of them had listened to God's word, yet perverted it after they had understood, and they were well aware."
11. Ibid, 2:87: "(...)Is it not often so, that whenever a messenger comes to you with that you yourselves do not desire, you become haughty, then accuse them of lying, and others you slay?"
12. Ibid, 2:51: "And (remember) when We appointed for Moses forty nights, and you took the calf (to worship) after him, for you were iniquitous."
13. Ibid, 2:61.
14. Ibid, 5:3: "(...)Today I have perfected your religion for you, and I have completed my blessings upon you, and I have approved for you Islam as religion.(...)"
15. Ibid, 2:41: "And believe in what I have sent down, confirming that which you already have (...)." Ibid, 2:121: "Those to whom We have given the Book and who read it in the right way, they believe therein (...)."
16. Ibid, 2:109: "Many of the people of the Book wish to bring you back to unbelief after you have believed, out of their own envy, even after the truth has become manifest to them (...)." See also A. Guillaume, *The life of*

Mohammad, A Translation of Ibn Ishaq's Sirat Rasul Allah, (London, 1955), p. 239.
17. FM, May 1990, p. 5.
18. Ibid.
19. Ibid.
20. The Islamists are not aware or do not want to acknowledge that the Kibbutzim were often socialist and not religious.
21. FM, May 1990, p. 6.
22. Ibid, p. 4.
23. Ibid, p. 6. Curiously, the Islamists equate the ultra-orthodox Jews with ultra-nationalism and thus overlook or suppress the principal rejection of the Jewish state by these groups.
24. FM, July 1990, p. 45.
25. Ibid.
26. Ibid.
27. Ibid.
28. The re-establishment of diplomatic relations with most of the former communist countries and the Soviet approval for the mass immigration of their Jewish citizens. FM, April 1990, p. 5.
29. Ibid.
30. FM, May 1990, p. 5.
31. FM, April 1990, p. 35.
32. FM, January 1990, p. 23.
33. FM, September 1990, p. 6.
34. FM, May 1990, p. 4.
35. *Mīthāq*, p. 23. This passage reveals clearly the influence of the most famous anti-Semitic forgery known as the "Protocols of the Elders of Zion" which circulated widely in the Arab world – as will be demonstrated later.
36. Ibid.
37. Qur'ān, 2:61 and 2:60; also 5:32.
38. Tafhīm, Vol. I, p. 99.
39. Qur'ān, 5:13: "(...)You will never cease to uncover treachery on their part, except a few of them (...)."
40. Ibid, 5:51: "O you who believe, take not the Jews nor the Christians for protectors, for they are protectors of one another. And whoever takes them for protectors shall be one of them (...)."
41. Ibid, 5:64.
42. Guillaume, op. cit., p. 437.
43. Ibid, p. 458.
44. Ibid, p. 246.
45. Ibid, p. 251.
46. Qur'an, 59:14. This point is made by Sayyid Qutb in "Our struggle with the Jews", translated in Ron Nettler, *Past Trials and Present Tribulations. A Muslim Fundamentalist View of the Jew*, (Oxford, 1987), p. 87.
47. Bernard Lewis, *Semites and Anti-Semites. An Inquiry into Conflict and Prejudice*, (London, 1986), p. 122.
48. FM, March 1990, p. 29.

49. FM, November 1990, p. 7.
50. FM, January 1990, p. 1
51. *Mīthāq*, p. 22.
52. Ibid.
53. Lewis, *Semites and Anti-Semites. An Inquiry into Conflict and Prejudice*, p. 199. A complete edition was officially issued in April 1956 in Cairo by the Egyptian Information Services. Today there are at least nine different Arabic translations on the market and the ideas of the "Protocols" were even introduced into school curricula. See Harkabi, op. cit., pp. 231, 236.
54. *Mīthāq*, p. 32.
55. Norman Cohn, *Warrant for Genocide. The Myth of the Jewish World-Conspiracy and the Protocols of the Elders of Zion*, (London, 1967), p. 22.
56. Ibid, p. 25.
57. Ibid, pp. 21–22.
58. Ibid, p. 23.
59. Harkabi reveals in *Arab Attitudes to Israel* the similarity of ideology between fundamentalists and Arab nationalists concerning the arguments for the struggle against Israel and the Jews as well as their characterisation.
60. In Beirut.
61. Ibid, p. 239.
62. Ibid, p. 26.
63. Ibid, p. 27.
64. Ibid, pp. 37,46,48.
65. See also Watt, *Islamic Fundamentalism and Modernity*, pp. 3–6.
66. Ibid, p.47.
67. Lewis, *Semites and Anti-Semites. An Inquiry into Conflict and Prejudice*, p. 132. One of the reasons for their anti-Semitism put forward by Lewis is the fact that the Jews represented commercial competitors to the Arab Christians as both groups were often involved in international trade.
68. Ibid, p. 197.
69. Ibid, p. 191.
70. FM, July 1990, p. 27.
71. Lewis, *Semites and Anti-Semites. An Inquiry into Conflict and Prejudice*, p. 196.
72. Ibid, p. 124.
73. Ron Nettler, *Past Trials and Present Tribulations. A Muslim Fundamentalist's View of the Jews*, (Oxford, 1987), p. 15.
74. Ibid, p. 21.
75. Ibid. Sayyid Qutb equates Jews and enemies of Islam including those who call themselves Muslims, but who harm in fact the Islamic creed. See Nettler's translation of "Our struggle with the Jews", pp. 76–77.
76. Harkabi, op. cit., p. 113.
77. Ibid, p. 299.
78. FM, April 1990, p. 25.
79. Ibid.
80. Ibid.
81. FM, April 1990, p. 26.

82. Ibid.
83. Joseph Nevo, "Zionism versus Judaism in Palestinian Historiography", unpublished draft, p. 10.
84. Ibid, pp. 5–6.
85. See: *The Encyclopaedia of Islam*, (Leiden, 1913).
86. FM, April 1990, p. 26.
87. Ibid.
88. FM, April 1990, p. 26.
89. Qur'ān, 2:256: "No compulsion is there in religion, for rectitude is henceforth distinct from perversity (...)." See also Chapter Six of this volume.
90. FM, April 1990, p. 35.
91. Ibid, p. 26.
92. FM, March 1990, p. 34.
93. Lewis, *Semites and Anti-Semites. An Inquiry into Conflict and Prejudice*, p. 213. Lewis argues that with the growing American influence in the world the racist became a fashionable enemy and thus Zionism became classified as racist. Ibid, p. 246.
94. FM, April 1990, p. 25.
95. Smith, op. cit., p. 110.
96. FM, April 1990, p. 25.
97. FM, July 1990, p. 31.
98. Guillaume, op. cit., p. 260. (*Ḥanīf* means "true believer".) See also Qur'ān 2:124: "And when His Lord tried Abraham with commands which he fulfilled, He said: I have made you an Imām (Leader) for the people (...)."
99. Generally this assertion refers to the Qur'ānic verse 2:125 even though the name Ka'ba is not mentioned: "And when We made the House a resort for people and a place of peace (...)." Mawdūdī includes the name Ka'ba in breaks in his English translation of the Qur'ān. See also Mawdūdī's interpretation of verse 2:146 ("Those to whom We have given the Book know him (the Prophet) as they know their own children, but a party of them conceal the truth, even though they know.") in his *Tafsīr*, Vol. I, p. 125: "The Jewish and Christian scholars were well aware that the Ka'ba had been constructed by Abraham ..."
100. FM, July 1990, p. 31. I could not find any *Ḥadīth* stating this.
101. Ibid.
102. FM, April 1990, p. 25.
103. FM, July 1990, p. 32.
104. Ibid.
105. FM, August 1990, p. 12. This is in fact an almost universal Arab position.
106. Ibid. The Islamists do not mention that this is equally true for Saudi-Arabia and Kuwait. On the other hand Israel did not employ workmen from outside before 1967 and this change of politics brought about an ideological crisis in Israeli society.
107. FM, April 1990, p. 24.
108. FM, July 1990, p. 27.
109. FM, April 1990, p. 35.
110. FM, March 1990, p. 35.

111. Ibid.
112. FM, July 1990, p. 29.
113. FM, August 1990, p. 29.
114. FM, July 1990, p. 9.
115. Ibid, p.8.
116. *Mīthāq*, p. 32. This expression is frequently used by Arab spokesmen and can even be found in Arab schoolbooks. See Harkabi, op. cit., p. 76. According to a story often repeated in Arab newspapers and books there is a map hanging in the Knesset which depicts Israel's aspiration for biblical borders. Ibid, p. 77.
117. *Mīthāq*, p. 32.
118. *Bayān Ḥamās*, 13.8.1990, in: FM, September 1990, p. 18.
119. FM, January 1990, p. 28 and ibid, March 1990, p. 39.
120. FM, July 1990, p. 1. It is a common Zionist argument that land should not be given back to achieve peace because this would only incite the Palestinians to ask for more. This is a nice example of how each side mirrors the other.
121. FM, January 1990, p. 3.
122. See Harkabi, op. cit., pp. 66, 68, 74.
123. Ibid, pp. 74, 82.
124. Ibid, p. 73.

CHAPTER THREE

The Goal: An Islamic Palestinian State

The goal of the Islamists is to liberate Palestine from occupation by the "Zionist enemy" and re-establish an Islamic state. With the Islamic conquest, Palestine – as any other land conquered by Islam – had become Islamic patrimonium or *waqf*[1] which does not belong to any person, party or state. It becomes the property of "former, present and future generations".[2] The people living on the land have been given the usufruct, but not the right of property.[3] Consequently no Arab state or leader nor any organisation has the right to make concessions on this land or to agree to the partition of it,[4] because who could possibly represent all Muslim generations from the creation until the Day of Judgement who collectively own the soil?[5] The recognition of the Jewish state in Palestine is considered *kufr*, meaning infidelity or unbelief.[6]

Palestine is said to have a special place in the Islamic creed[7] because Jerusalem had been the first direction of prayer for Muslims and the Al-Aqṣā mosque is considered the third sacred place of Islam. The Prophet had started his ascension to heaven from Jerusalem and his night-journey took him to Al-Aqṣā.[8] As Jerusalem and Palestine are presented as central to Muslims, it follows logically that their enemies throughout history tried to win Palestine in an attempt to defeat the Islamic *Umma*.[9] The Franks had fought for Palestine for 200 years and this attempt was repeated in World War I. Then the West decided to divide Palestine and to assure its permanent presence with the foundation of the "Zionist entity".[10] Thus Jerusalem has always been the "central point of the struggle between faith and unbelief"[11] and will remain the focus of this struggle. It is a fight between civilisations; the

West is trying to prevent the Islamic awakening.[12] It is therefore an individual's religious duty (*farḍ 'ayn*)[13] to fight for the liberation of Palestine and Jerusalem. There is no doubt about the advent of the "day of liberation" (*al-yawm al-taḥrīr*)[14] whose ideological content as well as its phonetical similarity seem to suggest that it equals the authors of the *Mīthāq* the "Day of Judgement" (*al-yawm al-akhīr*).

These arguments seem to be the most direct reflection of Qur'ānic revelation and Islamic tradition in the Islamists' thought. Even though the use of *waqf* for describing the land of Palestine seems to be a recent development, the idea underlying it has a long tradition: Any territory that is once "opened" (*maftūḥ*) to Islamic rule has to remain ruled by Muslims. As Muslims have to establish an Islamic society on earth, no territory can be left to non-Muslims to rule.[15]

Territory is thus important in Islam inasmuch as God's rule over it has to be established. This is an essential part of the Islamic venture on earth. But no territory was ever considered to be of a more central or sacred nature than another. In the Qur'ān only the holy towns of Mekka and Medina are mentioned. The notion of sacred territory is limited to the surroundings of these towns which non-Muslims are not allowed to enter. The al-Aqṣā mosque is venerated as a holy Muslim place, but the idea that the specific territory of Palestine is holy only emerged more recently. It certainly has no place in the fundamentalist ideology as developed by Sayyid Qutb and Sayyid Abul A'la al-Mawdudi who reject any attachment to a specific territory. Qutb clearly states that the notion of "territory" (*arḍ*) in Islam has only a value inasmuch as it "signifies the realisation of God's sovereignty and his rule over it".[16] The final goal can never be the protection and expansion of *Dār al-Islām*, but the spread of God's rule to the whole earth.[17] Mawdudi explains the change of the direction of prayer as a rejection of "chauvinistic attachment to blood and land".[18] Taking Jerusalem as the direction of prayer was a hard blow to the Arab "national vanity", the fixing of the Ka'ba as the direction of prayer alienated those worshiping the "idol of Israel".[19] Thus the attachment to a specific territory even for allegedly religious reasons is rejected by the ideologues of modern fundamentalism.

Ḥamās departs from its spiritual heritage on this issue. The Palestinian fundamentalists seem clearly to have been influenced by Judaism, in which the notions of the sacred territory and the promised land are prominent. As P. J. Vatikiotis notes, the Arab struggle for Palestine was from the beginning until 1967 based on a wider cultural Arab-Islamic identity, whereas that of the Jews always focused on territory.[20] Muslim identity is traditionally based on adherence to the religiously defined *Umma*; loyalty and membership are based on an ideological basis, not on a territorial one. Thus, throughout history Palestine had never been a separate entity, but was part of *Dār al-Islām*. As Hillel Frisch suggests, the "nationalisation of the universal religious doctrine of the Palestinian fundamentalist movement" is the result of emulation of the Jewish territorial doctrine of the "promised land".[21] The confrontation with the Jewish doctrine embodied in the state of Israel seems to have made necessary this innovation in traditional Islamic thought. In the concrete struggle against the Jewish state in Palestine the religious obligation to set up an Islamic society on earth might have been judged too general and abstract to challenge the very precise Jewish claims for the specific territory of Palestine. Thus we have another example of the emulation of foreign thought by the Islamists.

On the question of nationalism, *Ḥamās* makes an even more innovative and unorthodox move away from Islamic thought of the past. The Palestinian fundamentalists discarded the old incompatibility between Islam based on ideological grounds and the Western idea of the nation-state which is based on territorial claims: "Fatherland *(waṭan)* and nationalism (*waṭaniyya*) are (…) part of the Islamic creed".[22] "If nationalism means that certain people are linked through specific material, human and territorial characteristics, then this is the case of the Palestinian Islamic Resistance Movement".[23] But above all it has a "God that breathes soul and life" in it.[24] The use of the Qur'ānic image of the banner of God that "links the earth strongly to the sky"[25] seems to stand here for Palestine and Islam. As Palestinian nationalism is considered part of the Islamic creed, to give up any inch of Palestine would mean abandoning a part of the creed.[26]

These very surprising assertions lack all historical continuity with Islamic thought. The difficulty in finding any Qur'ānic evidence for these positions becomes clear when we examine the verses quoted in support: "(…) for rectitude is henceforth distinct from perversity. But whoever disbelieves in the *Ṭagh̄ūt* (evil) and believes in God, has firm hold of a strong handle that will not break (...)."[27] *Ḥamās* could hardly have chosen a more general, vague Qur'ānic directive to support its very specific position in the question of nationalism. Furthermore, the forefathers of the Islamist movement, Hasan al-Banna and Sayyid Qutb, never developed any theoretical basis for this. Even though al-Banna probably accepted implicitly the existence of nation-states as he was mainly active within the Egyptian society and political scene,[28] Mawdudi explicitly condemns any "national or racial vanity".[29] Any struggle for independence in this century was justified by Islamic groups in religious terms stating that the liberation of the respective country or administrative zone was a further step in the direction of one all-embracing Islamic entity. In *Ḥamās*' programme this "rhetoric" is less prominent; nationalism and the defence of a territorial homeland seem to have become more acceptable with time.

The Islamists' position on this question proves the extreme flexibility of their thought which integrates, with astonishing ease, ideas which had been considered incompatible for centuries. It seems that pragmatic reasons prevailed over traditional and ideological ones. An appropriate and efficient ideology for the struggle against the state of Israel was needed and some old hats had to be sacrificed. This pragmatism might be considered as characteristic for the movement.

The question of Palestine is furthermore preeminent in shaping the future of the Islamic *Umma*.[30] "The future of Palestine and the future of the *Umma* cannot be separated".[31] The Palestinian *Jihād* has positive consequences for the Islamic awakening[32] and the control over Palestine announces the control over the world.[33]

To understand the depth of this conviction, which could easily be taken as rhetoric, the role accorded to the history of mankind in the Islamic faith needs to be understood. Underlying the link between the establishment of an Islamic state in Palestine and the fate of the Islamic *Umma* is precisely this traditional perception of history as it emanates from the specific relationship between believer and God laid down in the Qur'ān. As Wilfred Cantwell Smith points out, the mediator between God and Man in Islam is righteousness (in Christianity it is the person of Christ).[34] Man approaches God by participating in the Islamic venture which is the realisation of the ideal society on earth. Smith emphasizes that a Muslim expresses his faith less in belief than in practical terms by behaving according to the accepted code. Thus the equivalent of the Christian "heresy" is in Islam "deviant" behaviour (*bid'a*).[35] Muslims thus have set out "to make history Islamic"[36] according to God's will. History is the arena in which God makes his will manifest through the believers.[37] The Muslim bears the full responsibility of making known to the world the validity of the Qur'ānic revelation.[38] The "motto" preceding the *Mīthāq* stresses this responsibility: "You are the best nation (*Umma*) that came forth to people, enjoining righteousness, and forbidding abomination, and believing in God (...)."[39] History therefore cannot be considered separately from the realm of the sacred.[40]

In contrast to Christianity, the formative centuries of Islam were characterised by conquests and temporal successes. The Islamic Empire soon stretched from North Africa to Asia. Since God leads those righteous believers who follow his plan for mankind to victory, salvation could be achieved through successes and achievement on earth.[41] The rapid expansion of the Islamic Empire confirmed the validity of the whole conception. Smith brought this characteristic feature of Islam into the short formula: "history confirmed faith".[42]

It now becomes clear why the Western domination of the Arab-Islamic world since the 19th century was felt to be such a catastrophe and a matter of shame. The incapacity of the Muslims to prevent the creation of a Jewish state in Palestine and the repeated military defeats against Israel had fundamentally undermined the self-confidence of Muslims and shaken the basis of their beliefs. The Muslims, representatives of God's will on earth, were defeated by the non-Muslim enemy. God had withdrawn his favour from the Islamic *Umma*. Historical events no longer corresponded to the divine plan given to the Muslims.

In Palestine, Muslims are fighting to reconcile history to Islamic beliefs and convictions. Thus the outcome of the struggle over Palestine is decisive for the whole *Umma*. A victory in this struggle would prove that Muslims are again on the right path and will continue to succeed in the world. This also means that the fight for Palestine can only be won under the banner of Allah – a fact proven largely by the historic examples of Muslim victories over the Christian crusaders and the

Tartars.[43] Muslims have to learn from their past experiences.[44] History is to be used as instruction.

The establishment of an Islamic state in Palestine is seen to be the only possible political solution: a state which will be part of a wider Islamic domain that will finally embrace the whole world.[45] *Jihād* is seen as the only means of spreading Islam to the four corners of the earth.[46] Even though the conflict is expressed mainly in Islamic terms, *Ḥamās* surprises the reader by the sudden introduction of Gamal Abd al-Nasser's three-circle-theory (*dawā'ir thalāth*) in a slightly modified form:[47] The liberation of Palestine has Palestinian, Arab and Islamic aspects and all three are essential to the struggle. Bearing in mind that Nasser – after a short honeymoon for tactical reasons – persecuted the Egyptian Muslim Brotherhood, this is even more astonishing. But the concept disappears as suddenly as it appears; the Qur'ānic verse quoted in support of this paragraph of the *Mīthāq* stresses only the importance of the al-Aqṣā mosque in religious terms.[48] We can only speculate about the meaning of this half-hearted excursion. Another attempt to widen the audience? This episode again demonstrates the extreme ease with which *Ḥamās* picks up "alien" ideas if tactically useful. It does not seem to fear protest from its followers as a result of the inconsistency.

Let me return to the proclaimed goal of an Islamic Palestinian state and how it should look. On this subject, indications are rare and vague. Only the geographical boundaries of the future state are clear. It comprises "Israel" and the so-called "Occupied Territories". There is no difference between Haifa and Einata, Nablus and Yaffa.[49] The Palestinian state stretches "from the river to the sea".[50] Jews born in Palestine will have the right to live there as they lived in the past in Islamic states,[51] which means as recognised religious minorities. Religious laws have to be respected by everyone. Laws issued by the people's deputies should be supervised by a religious committee for their compatibility with religious laws. If governments are too slow to implement laws and to ensure respect for them, then the people have to supervise their fellow-citizens.

The vagueness of this information reveals a characteristic feature of contemporary Islamists' thought. It never sketches a detailed picture of the Islamic state that should be established on earth. Only brief indications are made in passing.

NOTES

1. *Mīthāq,* p. 13.
2. FM, April 1990, p. 25.
3. *Mīthāq*, p. 13.
4. Ibid.
5. Ibid.
6. FM, September 1990, p. 21.
7. FM, July 1990, p. 27.
8. Qur'ān, 17:1.
9. FM, July 1990, p. 27.
10. Ibid.
11. Ibid.
12. FM, May 1990, p. 35.
13. *Mīthāq*, p. 16. See also Chapter Six of this volume.
14. *Mīthāq*, p. 16.
15. See Smith, op. cit., pp. 16–17.
16. Qutb, *Ma'ālim fī al-Ṭarīq*, 13th edition (Cairo, 1989), p. 85.
17. Ibid.
18. Tafhīm, Vol. I, p. 122.
19. Ibid.
20. P.J. Vatikiotis, *Islam and the State*, (London, 1987), p. 53.
21. Part of the title of Frisch's "The Case of Religious Emulation: The Nationalization of Universal Religious Doctrine in the Palestinian Fundamentalist Movement". In: *Middle East Focus*, Vol. 12 (3), Fall 1990, pp. 18–25.
22. *Mīthāq*, p. 14.
23. Ibid.
24. Ibid.
25. Ibid.
26. *Mīthāq*, p. 15.
27. Qur'ān, 2:256.
28. Reissner, Die militant-islamischen Gruppen, p. 473.
29. Tafhīm, Vol. I, p. 122.
30. FM, August 1990, p. 30.
31. FM, July 1990, p. 28.
32. Ibid.
33. FM, July 1990, p. 27.
34. Smith, op. cit., p. 17.
35. Ibid, p. 20.
36. Ibid, p. 18.
37. Yvonne Yazbeck Haddad, *Contemporary Islam and the Challenges of History*, (Albany, 1982), p. 6.
38. Ibid.
39. Qur'ān, 3:110. See explanation of this verse by Mawdudi, *Tafhīm*, Vol. I, p. 278.
40. Haddad, Challenge History, p. 5.

41. In strong contrast to the Christian salvation through suffering as represented by the symbol of the cross.
42. Smith, op. cit., p. 32.
43. *Mīthāq*, pp. 34–35.
44. Ibid, p. 35.
45. FM, May 1990, p. 35. This is one of the rare allusions to a wider Islamic entity.
46. FM, April 1990, p. 5.
47. *Mīthāq*, p. 16.
48. Qur'ān, 17:1: "Gloryfied is He who took His servant by night from the Sacrosanct Mosque to the Furthermost Mosque (...)".
49. FM, May 1990, p. 35.
50. FM, September 1990, p. 44.
51. FM, May 1990, p. 35.

CHAPTER FOUR

Sense of Urgency: Mass-Immigration of Soviet Jews

The injustice in Palestine has already lasted for more than forty years. The situation is as unacceptable today as it was in 1948 when Israel was established. In the eyes of *Ḥamās*, no progress has been made towards a solution. The Islamists have a very strong sense of urgency. Every day the enemy's state is established more firmly, the Western domination of the world-economy grows and the indoctrination of people's minds continues to make a return to Islam more difficult. On top of these evolutions, one major development, that nobody had foreseen, was a deadly threat to the Islamists' success: the mass immigration of Soviet Jews to Israel. *Ḥamās* felt that time was running out. A new situation was created. Only the Islamists acknowledged its fateful dimension.

The mass immigration of Soviet Jews to Israel[1] was repeatedly described as "the greatest danger" for the Palestinians.[2] It was seen as a "fateful issue in the struggle against the enemy".[3] The agreement reached between the USA and URSS was presented internationally as a proof of the URSS' respect for human rights.[4] In fact, it was yet another attack by the USA and the URSS against the *Intifāḍa* and the Arab countries. The Islamists drew one historical line from the Sikes-Picot-agreement (that divided the Middle East between the French and the British in World War I) and the Balfour declaration (promising the Jews a "Nationale Heimstätte" in Palestine in 1917) to this superpower-agreement. The betrayal of the Islamic *Umma* was seen to continue; the "world-wide Jewish conspiracy"[5] against the Muslims was at work again. The mass immigration was another attempt by the USA, the URSS and the Jews to determine the future of the Muslims by further spreading Western power in the heartland of the Islamic world.[6] The Islamists wondered if geo-strategic arguments did not play a role in this influx of people into the region, to allow Israel to get hold of the water resources of the region.[7] In any case, the massive influx of Soviet Jews increased the human potential of the "Zionist entity" and therefore increased its chance to win a military strike. The mass immigration thus augmented the danger that Israel would attack other Arab countries.[8] The first target would be Jordan which the Israelis have long imagined as an "*ersatz*"-homeland for the Palestinians.[9] "The *Umma* needs to defend herself",[10] she was again in a defensive position.

The emphasis on the urgent need to return to a true Islam is a "classical" theme of contemporary fundamentalist Islam. This feature becomes more prominent in Sayyid Qutb's later writing, mainly done in prison, when the conflict with Nasser's regime became irreversible and thus hope for gradual reform was definitively lost. Such a regime plunges society deeper each day into a state of *Jāhiliyya*. The salvation or "resurrection" (*ba'th*)[11] of the Islamic *Umma* thus became an urgent question.[12] This general fundamentalist theme of urgency was applied by the Palestinians to the very real threat of the mass immigration of Soviet Jews which created a new fait accompli: it strengthened Israel, making the possibility of a compromise on the Israeli side even more remote. The liberation of Palestine and the establishment of an Islamic state would thus be further postponed.

NOTES

1. 200,000 until January 1991.
2. FM, June 1990, p. 11; ibid, August, pp. 4–5.
3. FM, July 1990, p. 29.
4. FM, April 1990, p. 4.
5. FM, July 1990, p. 29.
6. FM, August 1990, p. 29.
7. Ibid.
8. FM, August 1990, p. 10.
9. FM, July 1990, p. 8.
10. FM, April 1990, p. 4.
11. Qutb, *Ma'ālim fī al-Ṭarīq*, p. 11.
12. "Humanity today is standing at the edge of the precipice". Ibid, p. 5.

CHAPTER FIVE

Hostility and Isolation

THE INTERNATIONAL COMMUNITY

The Islamists are very aware of the global dimension of our modern world. Regional issues are automatically tied to and depend on international constellations. Economic interdependence and dominance have their equivalents on the cultural and political level. However, the reality of power behind the present international system does not correspond to Islamic criteria; it is seen to be dominated by the USA and the West and is hostile towards the Muslim world; therefore the Islamists reject the legitimacy of the decisions taken by the existing international organisations.

The world is seen as divided into different peoples, nations, states, communities, religions and schools of thought that fight each other to gain influence and domination.[1] On an international level, states (*duwal*) and peoples (*shu'ūb*) are recognised as the main actors.[2] States are engaged in a permanent struggle for domination of the system with the militarily and economically stronger states fighting for the conservation of the status quo, whilst the weaker states of the Third World struggle to bridge the gap between themselves and the richer and stronger ones.[3] Thus the international system only understands the logic of power; the most powerful imposes its own interests while nobody protects the oppressed and the weak.[4]

The Islamists do not distinguish between Western capitalist and Eastern Communist powers, especially since Marxist ideology has crumbled in the East European countries and Western culture has been absorbed there.[5] "The West", as used by the Islamists, implies the main capitalist states, as well as the former popular democracies. Its common characteristic is its hostility towards Islam and its support for the "Zionist enemy".[6] This hostility is supported by the Qur'ānic verse "Believers! Do not take for intimate friends whose who are not of your kind.They spare no effort to injure you...".[7] In *Filasṭīn al-Muslima*, the Islamists explain in more detail what this unchanging attitude means in our contemporary world. The large powers seek control of the Arab world to which they attribute the leadership of the entire Islamic world.[8] By supporting the Arab regimes and opposing democratisation, the Western states prevent the Arab-Islamic world from developing its own force.[9] Moreover, since the surrender of the Eastern bloc, the Islamists consider the Third World to be the only power left to show the USA that the world is not its 51st federal state.[10]

The use of "the USA" as a synonym for "the West" is concordant with the view that the United States represents the head of the West, as it is its strongest power. Sometimes there is room for nuances and then Europe is seen as less unconditionally linked to the "Zionist entity" than the USA, but too weak to exert pressure on the USA.[11]

This political reality underlies the composition and work of the international organisations and at their head the United Nations Security Council. Therefore, the Islamists refuse to recognise their decisions.[12] They stress the accidental character of the existing international system which is a result of the second World War when the world was divided up between the victorious powers. Through the international organisations, those powers imposed their dominance not only on the defeated countries, but also on those which did not participate voluntarily in World War II. Today, the five members of the Security Council are the masters of the world and can veto any decision simply because they see it as a limitation of their influence. The gap between the rich north and the poor south widened over the years and the dominating powers want the poorest states to knock on the doors of the Western banks in order to get alms. It is obvious to the Islamists that this partition of the world and the organisation of the international community is evil. Thus they refuse to recognise the legality of the existing system and call for the construction of a new one, where relations between states are organised on a basis of justice (*'adl*) and equality of opportunity (*takāfu' al-furaṣ*).[13] The advanced states should be forced to give up their arrogance and to consider the interests of the other states; the rights of the oppressed throughout the world should be respected. In such a system, talks between the PLO and the USA would have the character of a real dialogue between partners of equal rights, instead of representing an "interrogation" (*istijwāb*)[14] of the PLO which can be interrupted whenever the USA has tactical reasons for doing so.

Consequently, *Ḥamās* does not believe in the usefulness of making complaints to the United Nations which is obviously dominated by "Western" interests. In the eyes of the Islamists, the Temple Mount massacre of October 8th 1990 had only torn the mask from the face of the USA. While the United States pretended to defend the weak (Saudi-Arabia) from the aggressor (Iraq), American arms delivered to Israel were used daily to kill Palestinians.[15] Not surprisingly, it took the UN five days of discussion to decide a "weak" (*hazīl*)[16] resolution concerning the Temple Mount massacre. Conversely, any resolution directed against the Islamic world is passed immediately. Thus, *Ḥamās* only trusts the help of God and its own force because nobody defends the al-Aqṣā mosque and the Muslim community.[17] The solution lies exclusively in the hands of the Palestinians and not in those of "any state in East or West".[18] At the same time, the PLO discredited its legitimacy as a representative of the Palestinian people by accepting the UN resolutions no 338 and 242 which were taken in the interest of the international community led by the USA.[19] In stronger terms: All UN resolutions are always directed by the enemy[20], meaning the USA and its "foster son" Israel (*rabīb*).[21]

Thus the stationing of US and other Western troops in Saudi-Arabia was considered another Christian attack (*al-hajma al-ṣalībiyya*)[22] on the *Umma*, and the UN approval of the use of force against Iraq was only a matter of form (*thawb jadīd*).[23] The former imperialist outlook on such actions was merely covered by a label more acceptable in the West: the USA claimed to defend justice and law in the name of the international community.[24] But the real interest and intention of the USA was to invade Iraq and thus to harm the Islamic *Umma*.[25] Since the UN resolutions only reflected the interests of the USA, the Islamic *Umma* could not recognise them and had to fight to preserve its independence and its own character.

The warning not to recognise the legality of the existing international organisations nevertheless does not advocate a break with the system or an end to participation in it.[26] In another context, *Ḥamās* even implores international Human Rights Organisations to intervene in the "Zionist" slaughter of Palestinians and their imprisonment.[27]

This apparently contradictory or at least ambiguous attitude of the Islamists towards the international system is derived from the contrast between their rejection of the "sanctification of its legitimacy" (*takrīs shar'iyyatihā*)[28] because of the existing power distribution and their acceptance of the idea of a "system of nations" (*al-niẓām al-dawlī*) itself.[29] They recognise the nation-state as the main actor on the international scene, even though there might be references to the Islamic *Umma* as a wider entity of solidarity. The term *al-dawla* is used abundantly and never questioned. It is the rulers of the states and the nature of relations between the states that is questioned. Based on the above mentioned "Islamic criteria" of justice and equality of opportunity, the international system of nation-states would be perfectly acceptable to Islamists and they do not propose a different organisation of the world. We could stretch this thought by arguing that the invocation of the solidarity of the Islamic *Umma* might often be used in order to establish these "Islamic criteria" in inter-Arab state-relations. It is not invoked to question the existence of those states.

Accordingly, the Islamists try to use the existing system to defend their interests. In the context of the feared mass emigration of Soviet Jews to Israel they stressed the need to put pressure on the USA, the USSR and the countries that played a mediator role in order to prevent this exodus. They even asked the Arab states to break their economic relations with the such states.[30]

The complaint that the UN never implemented any resolution on Palestine while they are immediately ready to enforce the resolutions on Kuwait[31] confirms the view that the Islamists are disappointed with the actual reality of power and interests ruling the international organisations rather than fundamentally questioning their existence on ideological or religious grounds.

But the Third World discourse about solidarity and equality in the international order is not all the Islamists have to say. They believe that the return to Islam in Muslim countries around the world can give rise to a power capable of overthrowing over the existing system and constructing a new order.[32] This order will first be based "on what is good for the Muslims" and assure the recognition of the Muslim countries as the leading power in the world.[33] The *Umma* has to be brought back to its assigned rank in the world.[34] This belief can be traced back to the Qur'ānic verses in which the Islamic *Umma* is described as the "best nation"[35] and Muhammad as the "seal of the prophets".[36] The finality of Islam which was brought to mankind by the last prophet, Muhammad, assures the superiority of the Muslims. This conviction is part of the traditional Islamic world view.[37] The innovation of the Islamists is the use of this element of the traditional world view in order to push Muslim leaders and people to play a more active role in world politics. To restore the Islamic *Umma* to the place in the world to which God had assigned it becomes a religious duty.

In this context, we can explain the extreme sensitivity to humiliation and indignity displayed by the Islamists. The frequent use of psychological vocabulary such as "feeling", "psychic forces" and "schizophrenia"[38] highlights their great sensibility in this area. The international system in its present power structure consistently subjects the Arab-Muslim world to degrading situations and poor treatment. The unilateral suspension of the talks between the PLO and the United States by the US-government after a Palestinian terrorist attack, which many PLO-leaders had condemned, was felt as a humiliation. The verbal detachment "was not enough to be worthy of the generous affection" of the USA.[39] The reaction of the USA was judged as a further confirmation of the conviction that "it is useless to bend in front of the USA and of Zionism".[40] Elsewhere the "arrogance" of the West (*al-gharb al-mustakbir*) was criticised and the importance of respecting the "feelings" (*wijdān*) of the oppressed people (*mustaḍ'afūn*) was underlined.[41]

The Islamists' position on the question of the international order clearly demonstrates one of the most characteristic features of their thought: it can be presented as traditional while also being innovative. Elements of the traditional Islamic world view, such as the superiority of the *Umma*, are used to push the Arab states to intervention, boycott and other modern means of influencing world politics. Furthermore, the religion-based discourse overlaps with a Third World discourse in which justice and equality should be the principles reigning over the international order. Weak states, their peoples and their feelings should be respected on equal terms by the leading Western industrial nations. This mixed discourse can easily serve as an "ideology" acceptable to a wider array of social forces.

THE ARAB-MUSLIM COUNTRIES

In the eyes of the Islamists, the situation is even worse than that. Not only is the whole world joined against Islam, but the *Umma* itself is fragmented, weak and does not play an active part in changing the world order. Solidarity among the Arab-Islamic countries is limited and the Palestinians feel their case has been abandoned by their Muslim brothers.

The Arab regimes are described as drowned in internal problems and geographical disputes with each other.[42] These quarrels prevent them from being strong enough to exert pressure on Israel and the West. They are incapable of coping with the current events and do not show any sign of activity on behalf of the Palestinian problem. The threat of the mass immigration of Soviet Jews to Israel has put this inactivity in the spotlight again.[43] The Arab countries failed to see that the Jewish mass immigration threatened them in the same measure that it strengthened Israel. The Palestinians alone have to pay the price for fighting the common enemy and for the transformation of the international order including the detente between Israel and the URSS.[44] The Arab regimes consider the Palestine problem as a "burden that should be resolved in any way".[45] While the East-Germans had the total support of the people, governments and rulers on the other side of the iron curtain when they pulled down the Berlin Wall, the Palestinians are applauded by nobody in their effort to pull down the "wall of occupation"[46] – not even by their Muslim brothers. The Palestinian Islamists repeatedly call on the Arab rulers and peoples as well as the media to support their struggle which is fought in the interest of all Muslims.[47]

But instead, the "regime of Camp David" (Egyptian leadership) hides itself behind the "American master".[48] It tries to manipulate other Arab rulers such as the Syrian and Libyan ones so that soon no real opponent to the US-position will be left.[49] While rich Arab states bring

69 million Arab Dollars to US-banks, the same states refuse six million Dollars financial help for the agricultural development of an non-oil-producing Arab country.[50] This evil situation of the Islamic *Umma*, its lack of solidarity, are the result of the despotic and unpopular rule present in most Muslim countries.[51]

The Islamists were shocked by the resentment and anger expressed against Palestinians in the Gulf-states after the PLO decided to support Saddam Hussein in the Gulf-crisis.[52] They claimed that the Palestinians in the Gulf-states were devoted to the development of their host-countries. At the same time, they expressed a more permanent disappointment about the treatment of Palestinians in the Gulf-states. Even after long years of service for their host-countries, the Palestinians had few rights and their children often did not have the right to go to government schools.[53] By contrast, foreigners in countries like Great Britain enjoy the same rights of education, health treatment and housing as regular citizens and they can attain British citizenship after five years.[54] Thus the Palestinians feel abandoned and betrayed by their Muslim brothers as well.

THE TRADITIONAL PALESTINIAN LEADERSHIP

The most bitter end is to come. The Palestinian people were not only abandoned by the surrounding Arab countries, they were even betrayed by their own leaders: "Certain Palestinian leaders" exploited the gains of the *Intifāḍa* by making concessions to American and Zionist claims.[55] They hoped thereby to get US-recognition and an international conference on the Palestinian issue.[56] Instead of taking their people by the hand and guiding them on the right path, those leaders pulled them onto the perilous ground of international alliances.[57] There could be no doubt that these indirect attacks were targeted at the leaders of the Palestinian Liberation Organisation.[58] Thus the foundation of *Ḥamās* was considered a blessed step (*khaṭwa mubāraka*)[59] as they were the only ones to defend the "real aspirations" (*taṭallu 'āt ḥaqīqiyya*) of the Palestinian people. This chapter has shown that the sense of isolation and betrayal of the Palestinian and Islamic cause is always present in the Islamists' mind. This feeling of being sold-out applies to the international order as well as to most Arab and even Palestinian leaders.

NOTES

1. FM, June 1990, p. 26.
2. Ibid.
3. Ibid.
4. FM, January 1990, p. 3
5. FM, September, p. 6.
6. *Mīthāq*, p. 24.
7. Qur'ān, 3:117; *Mīthāq*, p. 24; see Watt, *Islamic Fundamentalism and Modernity*, p. 98ff on the perception of the entire world as hostile to Islam which is going back to the times before the *hijra*.
8. FM, July 1990, pp. 10–11.
9. Ibid, p. 11.
10. FM, September 1990, p. 6.
11. FM, March 1990, p. 18; ibid, April 1990, p. 26.
12. FM, November 1990, p. 52. The following paragraph is entirely based on this article.
13. Ibid.
14. FM, August 1990, p. 4.
15. FM, November 1990, p. 7.
16. FM, November 1990, p. 52.
17. *Bayān Ḥamās* no. 65, in: FM, November 1990, p. 7.
18. FM, April 1990, p. 27.
19. FM, July 1990, p. 26.
20. FM, January 1990, p. 52.
21. FM, January 1990, p. 3.
22. FM, September 1990, p. 18.
23. Ibid.
24. FM, September 1990, p. 18.
25. Ibid.
26. FM, November 1990, p. 52.
27. FM, March 1990, p. 14.
28. FM, November 1990, p. 52.
29. Ibid.
30. FM, January 1990, p. 3.
31. FM, September 1990, p. 7.
32. FM, May 1990, p. 38.
33. FM, April 1990, p. 5.
34. FM, August 1990, p. 29.
35. Qur'ān, 3:110.
36. Qur'ān, 33:40.
37. See Watt, *Islamic Fundamentalism and Modernity*, pp. 4ff.
38. FM, March 1990, p. 11.
39. FM, July 1990, p. 1.
40. Ibid.
41. FM, November 1990, p. 52.
42. FM, March 1990, p. 2.

43. FM, August 1990, p. 29.
44. FM, March 1990, p. 2.
45. FM, March 1990, p. 2.
46. FM, January 1990, p. 6.
47. FM, July 1990, p. 8.
48. FM, September 1990, p. 6.
49. FM, August 1990, p. 5.
50. FM, September 1990, p. 6
51. See Chapter Six of this volume.
52. FM, November 1990, p. 2.
53. FM, November 1990, p. 3.
54. Ibid.
55. FM, January 1990, p. 2.
56. Ibid.
57. Ibid, p. 6.
58. I will discuss the relationship between the Islamists and the PLO at greater length in Chapter Eight.
59. FM, January 1990, p. 7.

CHAPTER SIX

Means

PALESTINE: *JIHĀD* IN FORM OF THE *INTIFĀḌA*

Confronted with the perceived isolation of their struggle on all levels, the only means to reach the proclaimed goal was *Jihād* – according to the Islamists' interpretation of the *Sharī'a*. It found expression in the form of the *Intifāḍa*. Strengthening this popular uprising was considered the only way[1] to successfully fight the Israeli occupation of Muslim territory and the world-wide Jewish conspiracy that was seen to be behind it.[2]

Any alternative way of finding a solution, such as an international conference with the participation of all concerned parties, was rejected. It seemed evident to the Islamists that the hostility overtly displayed by the international community would prevent any arrangement that was in the interests of the Palestinians. In other words: "Such a conference would merely place unbelievers in the position of arbiters over Islamic territory".[3] The Qur'ānic verse quoted in support of this inadmissible procedure illustrates the ease with which certain Qur'ānic ideas and verses can be used to express contemporary problems and feelings: "But neither the Jews, nor the Christians will be pleased with you until you follow their religion. Say: God's guidance is the real guidance. And if you follow their desires, after what has come to you as Knowledge, you will not have God as either helper, or protector."[4] This warning of the Qur'ān against the tricks and errors of his enemies can be transplanted without difficulty to the present day when the Arab-Islamic world finds itself on the defensive, facing Western cultural and political dominance. Any Palestinian concession to the interests of the Israeli state is equated with giving up belief in Islam by accepting Western (Jewish and Christian) standards. In a more general way, this Sura provides the perfect Qur'ānic support for the rejection of Western ideas and interests.

Thus the *Intifāḍa* was the only truly Islamic way of winning back Palestine. *Ḥamās* claimed to have started the uprising that broke out in December 1987 in refugee camps in the Gaza Strip.[5] It was *Ḥamās*-members who spread the movement to the West Bank.[6] Frequently, *Ḥamās* was described as the "head" of the *Intifāḍa* and thus of the Palestinian people, expressing and reflecting the will of the people.[7] In almost every interview, *Ḥamās*-leaders explained again and again that the organisation existed secretly before the 15th December 1987, but only came to the fore in January 1988. This tactic allowed the Islamists to stamp the *Intifāḍa* as an Islamic movement since its beginning. The spokesmen of *Ḥamās* in Gaza, Mahmud Zahhar, stressed the palpable growth of the Islamic movement during the *Intifāḍa*, pointing out that in 1990 there were over 200 mosques in the Gaza Strip.[8]

For the Islamists, there was no doubt that "the masses chose Islam as a programme for change".[9] The Islamic understanding of the conflict signified a way out of the impasse (*ma'ziq*) at which the struggle was stuck.[10] The Palestinian Islamists thus applied the fundamentalist principle that Islam is the only solution for all problems of contemporary Muslim societies. The Islamists admitted that since the outbreak of the *Intifāḍa* more Palestinians had been killed and arrested than before. Nevertheless, it was judged a success because it harmed the Israelis directly and physically. Thus the Israelis were forced to think it over "a thousand times" before they decided to settle in the Occupied Territories.[11] The Jews should learn that the *Intifāḍa* was a curse laying upon them until the Day of Judgement and that their end would come through the hands of the *shabāb* (the youth) of the Palestinian people.[12]

This return to Islam also explained why the movement could last successfully for so long against a much better equipped enemy and assured that it would continue until the final victory. The uprising sprang from the consciousness of every single Muslim and therefore it could not be stopped by anyone or any organisation.[13] Thanks to *Ḥamās*, the "real understanding of life" was spread among the Palestinians.[14] The *Intifāḍa* marked the Palestinians' return to Islam. The "Qur'ānic, godly" movement[15] revived the faith, brought the people closer to God and gave back to the loudspeakers of the mosques their true role.[16] Through this turn to Islam, the people returned to their "true nature and identity" after having followed different schools of thought.[17] Money and power no longer guided the Palestinians in their behaviour, but rather Islamic values prevailed such as solidarity and cooperation which could clearly be observed among families who had a member of their family killed or imprisoned.[18] The evils that brought grief to the Palestinians, such as "individualism, egoism, the absence of mutual help, the lack of tradition and the love of material values",[19] were eradicated.

These "evils" are in fact characteristics of modern society as such. This passage thus makes explicit an important aspect of the Islamists' ideology: it is partly directed against the "evils" of modern society which entered Palestinian society. The loss of identity, going along with the dissolution of traditional frameworks and relations, is in no way particular to Arab-Muslim societies. All European societies went through such a phase on their way to becoming modern industrial nations. But in the Palestinian case, this is certainly aggravated by the expulsion from the home territory, the shattering of the population and the constant denial of their identity by the Israeli occupying forces. The Islamic programme, fostering the restoration of traditional networks and social relationships, thus corresponds directly to the needs and aspirations of the people. At the same time, modernity can easily be identified with the state of Israel whose moral decadence is presented as threatening to the Palestinians. Thus the frustrations and feelings of insecurity about these societal changes can easily be channelled into the struggle against Israel.

The self-assertion due to an alleged return to traditional patterns of relationships and to the Islamic message bestowed the Palestinians with trust in themselves and in their capacity to change their fate.[20] They regained hope that they would not always be the loser.[21] This newly woken "will" (*irāda*) was seen as the driving force behind the *Intifāḍa*.[22] The changes started in the hearts of the people and therefore touched the whole of society. The main characteristic and strength of the *Intifāḍa* was the participation of the entire population, including children, women and old men.[23] In this sense, the Islamic *Intifāḍa* was characterised as a living model for all believing people of how to confront an enemy with the simplest weapons and *Ḥamās* claimed to be imitated by the Muslim brothers in Azerbaijan, Kashmir and even by the Chinese students.[24]

The *Intifāḍa* was presented as a form of *Jihād* which is considered to be the only means to liberate Palestine and to bring back glory to the Islamic *Umma*. At this point we have to scrutinise the Islamists' interpretation of *Jihād*, an often misused term which stands in modern Arabic for a rather vague concept.[25] "It is not the equivalent of war, which in Arabic might be rendered *qitāl*. *Jihād* has wider connotations and embraces every kind of striving in God's cause.[26] Thus *Ḥamās*' notion of *Jihād* is a typically fundamentalist interpretation which includes "struggles" like education or writing.

However, in another way, the Islamic Resistance Movement is departing from its fundamentalist spiritual heritage; it justifies the armed struggle as a reaction to the Israeli agression. In the *Mīthāq* we read that "the expulsion from the homeland (*waṭan*) is a kind of killing".[27] *Ḥamās* regularly explains that it had once been a purely political organisation, but "as the enemy closed all roads to a peaceful solution, the only means to realise this peace that remained was the use of our hands".[28] In this respect, *Ḥamās*' interpretation of *Jihād* is closer to a modernist's (apologetic) interpretation as a merely defensive war than to the explanation elaborated by the fundamentalist ideologue of Sayyid Qutb, who understood *Jihād* as an expansionist war in order to spread the Islamic *da'wa*. He vividly rejected the interpretation of modernist thinkers, like Muḥammad Abduh, who underline the defensive character of *Jihād* and only detect the duty to fight in the case of a foreign aggressor invading Islamic territory.[29] This is also the line of the late al-Azhār-Sheikh Maḥmud Shaltut's treatise on *Jihād*.[30] This piece was clearly written under the impact of the creation of the state of Israel in Palestine. Based on the interpretation of the Qur'ānic verse 2:191,[31] he underlines the duty to wage *Jihād* against those "expelling people from their homes, frightening them while they are safe and preventing them from living peacefully without fear for their lives or possessions".[32] This kind of persecution "is worse than persecutions by murder and bloodshed".[33] Muslims are thus "allowed to meet the hostility by the same means by way of retaliation".[34] Thus the modernist and *Ḥamās*' vision are completely concordant on this point. The right to *Jihād* in the Palestinian case is even admitted by the most defensive, apologetic trends in modern Islamic thought. The defensive aspect corresponds most directly to the situation in Palestine and thus *Ḥamās* uses it as a mobilising call.

By contrast, Qutb attacks the Westernised modernists as "spiritually and intellectually defeated people"[35] who search for "moral justifications"[36] for *Jihād*. He rejects their definition of it as a purely defensive war in reaction to an attack on Islamic territory.[37] For him, *Jihād* is a permanent situation of armed warfare, a natural struggle between two different consciousnesses.[38] The use of force against the unbelievers is an inherent duty in Islam, because the aim of Islam is to spread God's rule to the whole earth and among its entire population.[39] This does not imply the adoption of the Islamic creed by coercion,[40] merely the overthrow of systems and conditions that oppress and corrupt the individual.[41] "Those who claim that *Jihād* intends to defend Muslim territory, overlook the programme of Islam and consider it less important than territory (*waṭan*)".[42] In this phrase lies the key to the difference in thought between Qutb and *Ḥamās*; as we have seen before, the main innovation of the Palestinian Islamists' thought is their emphasis on homeland and nationalism, a logical result of the fact that the liberation of Palestine is the most preoccupying matter for all Palestinians. Thus their relationship to "territory" is different from the one of Qutb which leads to the emphasis of different elements in the struggle in God's path. For Qutb, the spread of God's rule on earth necessarily incudes the territorial expansion, but nevertheless this is secondary in his thought. For *Ḥamās*, on the other hand, the winning back of the lost homeland dominates all thought and represents in a way its *raison d'être*.

Thus we do not find any of the "classical" fundamentalist elaborations of the *Jihād*-doctrine in *Ḥamās*' publications – except the very general mobilizing call for action in the name of Islam. Almost the only Qur'ānic verse quoted in this context deals with the Jews' fear of fighting the Arabs.[43] Absolutely none of the Qur'ānic and *Ḥadīth* material quoted by Qutb is used by *Ḥamās*. This is a striking contrast to other domains such as the Islamists social doctrine in which *Ḥamās* repeats Qutb's thought almost word for word. These divergences of thought and of emphasis have to be seen in their contrasting historical contexts. When Qutb was writing his main works in the 1950s and 1960s, Egypt was an independent state and there was no more need for a mobilizing doctrine to fight foreign invaders. Furthermore, Qutb was mainly a theoretician, whereas *Ḥamās* is a militant organisation fighting a battle.

As we have seen before, *Ḥamās* views the fight for the liberation of Palestine as an "individual religious duty" (*farḍ 'ayn*)[44] which even allows wives to fight the enemy without the permission of their husband and slaves without the permission of their master.[45] Any Muslim who avoids fighting is committing "major treason" accordingly to the Qur'ān.[46] This interpretation contrasts with Sunni mainstream thought in which *Jihād* is traditionally considered by "all jurists, with almost no exception"[47] as a collective rather than individual obligation (*farḍ kifāya*) binding the whole Muslim community as a collective group. The duty is fulfilled when a part of the community fulfills it.[48] Women, disabled persons and old men are normally exempt from the duty to go to battle.[49] Only the Kharijites made the individual obligation a pillar of faith. In classical *fiqh*, *Jihād* becomes a personal duty only in some special cases, mainly when the enemy attacks Islamic territory. All inhabitants of the territory – including women and slaves – are then obliged to expel the enemy.[50] Ibn Rushd holds that *Jihād* becomes an individual duty when there is nobody else [no organised state army] to carry it out.[51] So the exceptional and peripheral regulation of the Qur'ān and classical *fiqh* for *Jihād* as an individual duty becomes the central pillar of the contemporary Islamists legalistic-religious framework.

Another aspect of *Ḥamās* notion of *Jihād* is the fact that "the Islamic *Umma* is only completely united and concentrates all its forces when it finds itself in trenches and harbours [= war, struggle] and history is the best proof for this".[52] This passage indicates that the *Jihād* for the liberation of Palestine serves at the same time the purification of the *Umma*. "But We fling the truth against mendacity; so it discomfits it and causes mendacity to perish."[53] It compels Muslims to put all their energy into the battle, thus bringing them automatically back on the path of Allah and saving them. We could also put it the other way round: the enemy can only be beaten if the Muslims fight in the path of Allah, as history has shown in the victories over the Crusaders and the Tartars.[54] In this way human civilisation had been saved in the past.[55]

This significance of *Jihād* for the purification of Muslim society confirms that it is more than just military fighting; the starting point for both is the spread of the Islamic consciousness.[56] Thus the intellectual elites are called to contribute to the *Jihād* by writing books and articles educating Muslims in this consciousness.[57] Women play no more minor role than men as they give birth to new Muslims and prepare them for the *Jihād*.[58] Thus the role of women in the *Jihād* is to be good Muslim mothers who instill their children with religious values and duties.[59] The emphasis on Islamic education is characteristic for fundamentalist thought in this century. The fundamentalists' harsh criticism of the religious establishment was mainly directed against what was seen as the failure of the *'ulemā'* to assure true Islamic education. Thus *Ḥamās* is worried about the closing of schools and universities in the Occupied Territories. This is a particularily serious problem as about half the Palestinian population is under fifteen years old. The Islamists propose to exempt schools from strike calls in order to prevent their closure by the Israelis.[60] In the realm of art, the Islamists call for the creation of Islamic art. "Men do not only consist of clay, but they have a soul."[61] Islamic art can mobilize thought and feelings.[62] This very broad vision of *Jihād* corresponds to the fundamentalists' vision of Islam as a force comprising all areas of human life.

Concerning the military struggle, Sheikh Yassin stressed in 1990 that until then no children, women or old men had been killed.[63] Thus the classical rules and regulations of *Jihād* laid down in the Qur'ān and in Islamic law were accepted as binding for the *Intifāḍa*. Important Traditions prescribe that these categories of the enemy people must be spared.[64] At the same time, Sheikh Yassin compared the Palestinian *Jihād* with the Jewish resistance against the British Mandate force which nobody considered as terrorists.[65] "We are not murderers as the Western media present us", said another article.[66]

Here we have another example of how the Islamists feel compelled to explain their cause according to two different standards, the Arab-Muslim one and the Western one. While the *Intifāḍa* is praised as *Jihād* for one public, it is "justified" as a liberation struggle to the other audience. Fully aware of the importance of Western media, they have to "sell" and defend their action in terms acceptable to the Western public. They are conscious that the reference to *Jihād* – which can easily have a mobilizing effect on Arab-Muslim people – raises the fear and incomprehension of the Western public that equates it with brutal aggression.

THE ARAB-MUSLIM WORLD: ISLAMIZATION AND DEMOCRATIZATION

According to *Ḥamās*, the *Intifāḍa* can also serve as an example for the other Arab-Muslim countries of the region that are not occupied by foreign forces, but which are nevertheless weak and fragmented. The strength of the *Intifāḍa* was that it had the participation of all fragments and layers of the population. This confirmed its Islamic character, since Islam is the "real nature" and identity of the people. At the same time, it represented the will of the people and therefore was a form of democracy. This is what is needed in the Arab countries today.

The Islamists state the weakness of the Arab states and their inner-Arab quarrels which prevent them from procuring for the *Umma* the rank it deserves on the international scene. Looking into the future, Islamists are frightened because they see a worsening of the situation, a further weakening of the Islamic *Umma*.[67] The Gulf crisis had again thrown light on the gap between governments and people in the Arab world. It had also made clear the extent to which many regimes obey the USA.[68] These two characteristics are closely linked in the minds of the Islamists.

Most of the present regimes are regarded as dictatorships (*dīktātūriyya*) which are based on "oppression" (*qama'*) and a single-party-rule (*niẓām al-ḥisb al-wāḥid*).[69] The will of the ruler is supreme law and any opposition is rejected as ungrateful and is persecuted.[70] The main goal of this type of government is to uphold the fear of the state and its order, personified in the ruling figure.[71] The preeminent feature of this relation between ruler and ruled is "the absence of the will of the people (*taghayyib lī-irādat al-jamāhir*), the ignorance of their hopes and dreams" which the dictatorial regimes (*diktātūriyyāt*) of the region rule over and with which they play.[72]

The oppression of Islamic groups and parties in many Arab countries is a further proof of the dictatorial nature of the regimes. The Libyan leader, Colonel Kadhafi, was blamed severely for his oppression of the Islamic opposition to his rule which "undermines human rights".[73] *Filasṭīn al-Muslima* emphasised that it did not invoke human rights in order to please human rights organisations, but for the sake of uniting Muslims confronted with external challenges.[74] Regarding the difficulties of the Islamists in Tunisia and supporting the beginning of democratisation in Algeria and Jordan, it was affirmed that "democracy is bound to rule in our countries sooner or later"[75] and that there is no "democracy without Islamists" (*dīmuqrāṭiyya bilā' islāmiyyn*).[76]

Another example of the dictatorial character of many Arab regimes is the submissiveness of the Arab press.[77] The lack of freedom of press is denounced as the "missing fact" (*al-ḥaqīqa al-ghā'iba*).[78] The hopes of certain Arab regimes to be considered as democratic simply because of their opposition to Saddam Hussein in the Gulf crisis are rejected.[79] The Islamists affirm that they cannot be fooled: "The majority of the present Arab regimes are of a dictatorial nature."[80] Thus the Islamists address themselves directly to the people. They appeal to the "citizens and responsibles" of the Gulf states and Saudi-Arabia to recognise the Palestinian participation in developing their respective countries.[81]

There is no doubt for *Ḥamās* that the "real nature" (*al-huwiyya al-ḥaqīqiyya*) of the Muslim people is the longing for a democratic form of rule.[82] Islam is also part of the "true nature" of Muslims and thus a greater participation of the population will lead to an Islamisation of state affairs. This concept of development closely follows the "classical theory" of contemporary Muslim fundamentalism in saying that the Islamic values first gain the soul of the individual Muslim; then a growing nucleus of true believers will gradually transform society and state.[83] Thus the liberation of the people's will (*taḥarrur irādat ayy sha'b muslim*) is seen as a major step (*khaṭwa 'asāsiyya*) towards the liberation of the Holy Land (*taḥarrur al-arḍ al-muqaddasa*).[84] The call for the implementation of the *Sharī'a* accompanies the demand for democracy, the successful fusion of both is exemplified in the *Intifāḍa*-movement.

Another example is Algeria where the "glorious *Intifāḍa*" of 1988 "changed the power-balance in favour of the people" and created a new relationship between state and society (*mujtama'*).[85] The developments threatening the Arab-Muslim world, such as the Jewish mass immigration or the re-establishment of diplomatic relations between Israel and East European countries, can only be faced efficiently if the relations between governments and people are renewed and based on cooperation and solidarity.[86] In the present relationship between the rulers and the ruled in the Arab world this is impossible.

This section deals with one of the most interesting features of the Palestinian Islamists' thought, the link between Islam and democracy. But what do they understand by "democracy" and what are the concepts underlying their vision of it? First of all, we have to note that the Islamists' harsh attacks on the existing Arab regimes were only possible on the ideological ground prepared by former fundamentalist thinkers. Sayyid Qutb, the "first ideologue of radical Islam",[87] elaborated a comprehensive ideology for Sunni rebellion against authority. He reinterpreted the notion of *Jāhiliyya*, stressing that it does not denote a precise period in history, but a situation that occurs every time a society strays from the Islamic path.[88] It signifies essentially the return to "human arbitrariness" (*ahwā' al-insān*) as a supreme source for rule and legislation by leaving aside God's programme and legislation.[89] In this category, Qutb includes the legislation made by a single person, by a group or class of society and by a group of nations.[90] All these procedures are *Jāhiliyya*. The answer to such behaviour can only be rejection and rebellion. Muslims can only practice their Islam in a Muslim milieu where Islam is sovereign; otherwise they are part of a *Jāhiliyya* society. Thus Qutb justifies rebellion against the ruler in the name of Islam and ends a tradition of quietism – or, as P. J. Vatikiotis puts it, he introduced a "contractual theory of government" into Islamic political discourse which makes dissidence and rebellion possible.[91]

But Qutb's theory takes a different form in the hands of Palestinian fundamentalists hands. They never use the term *Jāhiliyya* and only rarely denounce the rulers for not being "real" Muslims. Instead they denounce the "dictatorial" nature of most of the existing Arab regimes which oppress the people, especially the Islamist groups, and spoil their countries' resources. Thus the "will of the people" should govern the state, at least on an equal level with the will of God. This idea is absolutly incompatible with the fundamentalist Islamic concept – as only in the 1950's defended by Qutb – that popular sovereignty cannot be at the basis of legitimate authority because all sovereignty belongs to God. Muslims are his vice-regents on earth, executing his orders, not representatives of other men. These incompatible views are fused with an incredible ease and not even discussed. There is no theoretical elaboration of this major innovation. The vocabulary used reveals the origin of these new influences. The Islamists use mainly terms of Western political sciences to formulate their opposition and criticism: *dimūqrāṭiyya* and *diktātūriyya*, the will of the people (*irādat al-sha'b*). This illustrates a major departure from classical Islamist thought which removes one of the main obstacles to the introduction of a form of Western democracy in Muslim countries. However, the absence of discussion of this major innovation makes it doubtful how deep-rooted this conviction is.

It seems, rather, that this is another example of the Islamists' need to make their arguments satisfy Islamic and Western liberal standards simultaneously. The concept of *Jāhiliyya* elaborated by Qutb underlies the criticism of Arab regimes, but it is mainly expressed by invoking the principles of Western democracy. One can again detect the apologetic element of modern Islamist thought. In Ameer 'Ali's book *The spirit of Islam*, a classical example of Islamic liberalism defending Islam against Western accusations, we can read that Muhammad preached the "new democracy".[92] This argument is mainly based on the Islamic idea of the equality of men. But as we will see later, in the chapter on religious minorities, the Islamic idea of the equality of men is different from the Western notion: religious minorities are not equal to Muslims.

One might speculate that the Islamists' call for democracy is a tactical manoeuvre because in the current political situation in the Arab-Islamic world free elections might assure them the ascendancy to power. And as easily as it was integrated into their thought it might be rejected again if the political situation changes. This could be true, even though Islamists probably do not see it in these terms. As I have shown in the preceding section on the *Intifāḍa*, the Islamists genuinely believe that Islam corresponds to the "true nature" of Muslim people. If Muslims stray from their path and adhere to other ideologies, this is only a matter of ignorance and it is hoped that one day this "true nature" will regain the upper hand. The Islamists can thus be very confident and honestly support the idea of free elections.

Their idea of democracy seems to include free elections which will express the people's will, but not necessarily political pluralism and conflict. The "will of the people" seems to be understood as a monolithic bloc which might not be in agreement with the rulers. The conflict is perceived between the people and the ruler, and conflicts within this "will of the people" are rarely mentioned. The conviction that their understanding of Islam is the only possible one makes *Ḥamās* believe that there cannot be any disagreement among true believers. A clear example of this thought is the statement of *Ḥamās* saying that all Muslims following the Islamic programme are automatically part of *Ḥamās* and cannot possibly adhere to another Islamic group.[93] At another occasion they underline their respect for other Islamist groups "as long as their behaviour remains within the boundaries of Islam".[94] It is likely that the Islamists are the only ones authorized to define those boundaries of truly Islamic behaviour; Islam is thus narrowed down to their understanding of Islam. They make clear that they won't accept any "challenge (*ṭa'n*) or denouncement (*tashhīr*) of individuals or the community, because believers never defame nor curse".[95] Individuals are thus denied the right to criticise. In a rather autocratic way, the Islamists appoint themselves as judges over the community by insisting on *Ḥamās*' right to criticise and to point out faults.[96] This is a rather free interpretation and inversion of the Qur'ānic verse endorsing this position: "God loves not public avowal of evil words, save he who has been wronged.(...) If you do good openly, or conceal it, or pardon evil, then God is Forgiving, Omnipotent."[97] Mawdudi explains these verses as a moral directive given to the Muslims when Jews and hypocrites persecuted them and thus roused their anger. Following the example of God, Muslims should be generous in spirit and full of tolerance towards their enemies.[98] The militant Islamists, convinced of the exclusive truth of their vision of Islam, display little tolerance even towards fellow Muslims. Their monolithic vision of Islam does not allow this. Consequently, they do not develop any tools for coping with dissent among the people. Many elements, then, point out that the Islamists' vision of democracy is quite different from the one developed in Western Europe, even though the same terminology is used.

NOTES

1. FM, March 1990, p. 35; *Mīthāq*, p. 15.
2. FM, July 1990, p. 29.
3. *Mīthāq*, p. 15.
4. Qur'ān, 2:120.
5. See interview with Jamal Hamami, one of the leading figures of *Ḥamās*, in FM, June 1990, p. 10.
6. Ibid.
7. FM, August 1990, p. 5.;
8. FM, March 1990, p. 10.
9. FM, April 1990, p. 46.
10. FM, March 1990, p. 10.
11. FM, March 1990, p. 3.
12. FM, January 1990, p. 1.
13. FM, June 1990, p. 10.
14. FM, August 1990, p. 11.
15. Letter from an Indian Muslim in FM, March 1990, p. 29.
16. FM, January 1990, p. 10.
17. FM, September 1990, p. 10. One of the examples given: Instead of serving imported Nescafé to visitors, the Palestinians offer fruit from their own gardens. See FM, September 1990, p. 39.
18. FM, April 1990, p. 10.
19. FM, September 1990, p. 37.
20. FM, January 1990, p. 10.
21. FM, March 1990, p. 10.
22. FM, September 1990, p. 37.
23. FM, March 1990, p. 10.
24. FM, March 1990, p. 1.
25. Rudolph Peters, *Islam and Colonialism. The Doctrine of Jihad in Modern History*, (The Hague, 1979), p. 3.
26. Mawdudi, *Tafhīm*, Vol. I, p. 169.
27. *Mīthāq*, p. 22.
28. FM, March 1990, p. 35.
29. Peters, *Islam and Colonialism. The Doctrine of Jihad in Modern History*, p. 126.
30. Translation of his treatise "The Qur'ān and Fighting" in Rudolph Peters, *Jihad in Medieval and Modern Islam*, (Leiden, 1977), pp. 26–80.
31. "And kill them wherever you find them, and eject them from places whence they ejected you, for sedition is worse than carnage.(...)"
32. Peter's translation in *Jihad in Medieval and Modern Islam*, p. 44.
33. Ibid.
34. Ibid, p. 44. This position is based on the Qur'ānic verse 2:194: "So, whoever commits aggression against you, attack him in like manner as he attacked you..."
35. Qutb, *Ma'ālim fī al-Ṭariq*, p. 72.
36. Ibid, p. 82.

37. Ibid, p. 73.
38. Ibid, p. 86.
39. Ibid, p. 85.
40. Ibid, p. 83.
41. Ibid, p. 89.
42. Ibid, p. 84.
43. The Qur'ānic verse 59:13 is quoted in the *Mīthāq*, p. 12: "Indeed fear of you is more intense in their hearts than of God. That is because they are people who comprehend not."
44. *Mīthāq*, p. 14, p. 16.
45. Ibid.
46. *Mīthāq*, p. 32. The Islamists quote verse 8:16 to make this point: "And he who turns his back to them [unbelievers] that day, unless manouvering for battle or intending to join another (part of his) host, he is laden with wrath from God and his abode shall be in Gehenna (...)."
47. Majid Khadduri, *War and Peace in the Law of Islam*, (Baltimore, 1955), p. 60. See also in this sense Ibn Rushd in Peters, *Islam and Colonialism. The Doctrine of Jihad in Modern History*, pp. 9–10.
48. Qur'ān, 9:112; Khadduri, op. cit., p. 60.
49. Khadduri, op. cit., p. 85. Peters, *Islam and Colonialism. The Doctrine of Jihad in Modern History*, pp. 15–17.
50. Peters, *Islam and Colonialism. The Doctrine of Jihad in Modern History* p. 15.
51. See Peters translation in *Jihad in Medieval and Modern Islam*, p. 10. See also the story of a Muslim woman killing a Jew who is spying around her house while there is no man at home. Guillaume, op. cit., p. 458.
52. FM, April 1990, p. 24.
53. Qur'ān 21:18, quoted in the *Mīthāq*, p. 8.
54. *Mīthāq*, p. 30, p. 34.
55. Ibid, p. 30.
56. *Mīthāq*, p. 17. This is the main pillar of the system of thought developed by Sayyid Qutb.
57. *Mīthāq*, p. 30.
58. *Mīthāq*, p. 19.
59. *Mīthāq*, pp. 19–20.
60. FM, June 1990, p. 3.
61. *Mīthāq*, p. 21.
62. Ibid.
63. FM, March 1990, p. 35.
64. See Ibn Rushd in Peter's translation in *Jihad in Medieval and Modern Islam*, p. 16.
65. FM, March 1990, p. 35.
66. FM, May 1990, p. 39.
67. FM, August 1990, p. 29.
68. FM, September 1990, p. 7.
69. FM, November 1990, p. 14.
70. Ibid.

71. Ibid.
72. FM, September 1990, p. 4.
73. FM, September 1990, p. 12.
74. Ibid.
75. FM, September 1990, p. 13.
76. Ibid.
77. FM, November 1990, p. 13.
78. Ibid.
79. FM, November 1990, p. 14.
80. Ibid.
81. Ibid, p. 3.
82. *Bayān Ḥamās* no. 62, 13.8.1990. In: FM, September 1990, p. 18.
83. FM, April 1990, p. 5.
84. FM, July 1990, p. 11.
85. FM, July 1990, p. 13.
86. FM, July 1990, p. 11.
87. Vatikiotis, op. cit., p. 63.
88. Qutb, *Ma'ālim fī al-Ṭarīq*, p. 224; See also Qutb, *Fī Ẓilāl al-Qur'ān*, p. 891. The concept of *Jāhiliyya* and his vision of *al-niẓām al-islāmī* are elaborated in his exegesis of the Qur'ānic verses 5:45–50.
89. Ibid.
90. Ibid. Qutb thus attacks international organisations like the United Nations.
91. Vatikiotis, op. cit., p. 67.
92. Ameer 'Ali, *The Spirit of Islam. A History of the Evolution and Ideals of Islam*, (London, 1922), p. 204.
93. FM, September 1990, p. 8.
94. *Mīthāq*, p. 25.
95. Ibid.
96. Ibid.
97. Qur'ān, 4:148–149.
98. Tafhīm, Vol. I, p. 101.

CHAPTER SEVEN

Self-Image of Islam

As I have discussed, *Ḥamās* perceives Islam in a defensive position, struggling against a local as well as an international environment that is openly hostile towards Muslims. The *Umma* has to be protected from threatening developments such as the mass immigration of Soviet Jews to Israel. The Islamic world is seen to be in a deep crisis. Nevertheless, the Islamists display self-assurance, optimism and belief in the final victory.

In the eyes of *Ḥamās*, whose members are "Muslims respecting the Qur'ān and the Sunna", "it cannot be difficult or impossible" to overcome the present crisis and weakness of the Islamic world.[1] Muslims have always to remember that Islam is the "best godly message for mankind".[2] Despite all setbacks they never should lose the conviction "that they are in the possession of the welfare for the entire mankind".[3] The victory of the Islamists in Jordan, where they won 31 parliamentary seats in 1989, constitutes a "clear message to enemy and friend",[4] "Islam is advancing inevitably and this religion experiences a new birth, no matter how difficult and painful this is".[5] "Islam will win in the end".[6] Western countries are asked in their own interest "not to spoil things with the Islamists",[7] as they will be in power one day.

Ḥamās makes these confident predictions, even though they believe that no human being can predict the future – the best proofs for this are the surprising events in Eastern Europe since 1988.[8] Predictions are nevertheless possible if they are based on the Qur'ān and the Sunna. "The Qur'ānic prophecy is true and decisive".[9] Thus certain prognostics can be made such as "the victory of faith over unbelief, the disappearance of Israel, the fall of both communism and capitalism, the end of the hegemony of the URSS and the USA and finally the victory of the Islamic revolution".[10] These predictions do not include the announcement of an exact hour and place.[11]

The Islamists make clear that this knowledge should not lead to a fatalist, passive attitude towards life and achievement. They emphasise that "God gave reason, will and consciousness to man as well as to states and nations"[12] in order to use it. *Ḥamās* stresses in the *Mīthāq* that "every man is responsible before God",[13] quoting as a proof the *Sūrat al-Zalzala*.[14] For fighting the mental and military invasions of the West and Zionists, Muslims are told to learn from past historical experiences because this is not incumbent upon Allah.[15] This does not mean that man's capacities are not ultimately restricted by the power and might of Allah.[16]

This appeal to the personal consciousness and responsibility of Muslims indicates that *Ḥamās* has an activist Islam in mind. This is a very important feature of modern Islamic thought. Struggling for change – change in the sense of forming a society and state according to their understanding of Islam and the early Muslim community –[17] the Islamists fight the fatalist aspects of Islam. Though they appeal to the Muslim *Umma* as a whole, at the same time they address their calls directly to the individual believer. We have seen this emphasis on the individual in the Islamists' call for *Jihād*. The emphasis on the individual clearly emanates from the fundamentalists' conviction that the "return" to "true" Islam can only be achieved through the conversion of the individual Muslim's mind and heart. Thence the importance of education in all fundamentalist thought. At the same time, this appeal to the individual corresponds to the principles of modern politics in which the broad population is supposed to participate through their participation in mass organisations. The Muslim Brotherhood in Egypt had been one of the first mass movements in the Islamic world and this popular nature is still a characteristic of the fundamentalist movement today.

This notion of popular activism might contribute to the confidence displayed by *Ḥamās*. The other sources of confidence are the ideas of the finality of Islam and its self-sufficiency which are pillars of the traditional Muslim world-view.[18] Based on the Qur'ānic verse in which Muhammad described as the "seal of the prophets",[19] Muslims believe that he was the last prophet and that Islam is the eternal godly message. Islam must therefore be victorious. This view is confirmed by the verse saying that the Islamic *Umma* is the "best nation".[20] These traits of the traditional self-image of many Muslims fit perfectly well with the often observed need for the assertion of a society on the defensive: The statements of confidence and the superiority of Islam serve as a compensation for the obvious weakness of contemporary Arab-Muslim societies.

Ḥamās' vision of the "true" Muslim who struggles fiercely for the realisation of the Qur'ānic prophecy, driven by the promise of the final victory, is best reflected in the numerous portraits of Sheikhs leading armed struggles for the liberation of the oppressed Muslim people. The greatest idol of the Palestinian Islamists is without doubt Sheikh Izz al-Din al-Qassam after whom the military wing of *Ḥamās* is named. "The Qur'ān and the rifle" is the title of one of his portraits.[21] Convinced of the superiority of the Islamic message, he organised an armed revolt against British and Zionist oppressors in Palestine in the forefront of the Great Palestinian Rebellion of 1936–39. He was killed in 1935. The resistance activities of the limbe Sheikh Yassin, the head of the Muslim Brotherhood and *Ḥamās* in Gaza, is another example of regular praise.[22]

The heroic portrait of the Azhar-learned Dr. Abd Allah Azzam[23] painted in *Filasṭīn al-Muslima* leads us again to the international dimension of Islam: The praised *'ālim* died in November 1989 as a martyr (*mujtahid*) in Pakistan where he supported the Afghan *Mujāhidūn*. Of Palestinian origin, he had studied in Cairo, then went to Jordan to participate in the Palestinian *Jihād* from 1968 to 1970. After teaching for a time in Saudi-Arabia, he went to Pakistan and joined the Afghan *Mujāhidūn* there. *Ḥamās* constantly stresses the international dimension of Islam. In *Filasṭīn al-Muslima* this is reflected by regular reports on other Muslim countries and the situation of the Islamist movement there. They put the Palestinian-Israeli conflict, even though it is central to the Islamic cause, into a wider framework, it is part of the oppression of Muslims throughout the world. The only means to fight this unacceptable situation is international Islamic cooperation. This is the only way to encounter the world-wide Jewish conspiracy against Islam. Again the Islamists' ideas seem to be a direct reaction to the enemy's behaviour, the world-wide Jewish network and organisations seem almost to be taken as an example. The Muslim Brotherhood, of whom *Ḥamās* claims to be the Palestinian branch, represents exactly the type of international Islamic network which the Muslim world needs so badly.

Another aspect of Islam emphasised by *Ḥamās* is its social component. The Muslim Brotherhood since its inception in Egypt in the 1920s focuses on charity work and social services and *Ḥamās* is born out of this tradition. The Islamists call for solidarity and cooperation among peoples and states instead of the policy of strength which operates in the existing international order dominated by the West. While the people of Arab-Muslim countries are in general referred to as the "oppressed", the "weak" and the "poor", the "Zionist enemy" is supported by the world-wide Jewish "bourgeoisie".[24] As I have previously mentioned, the Islamists use "Islamic countries" and "the Third World" interchangeably.[25] But the Islamists' demands are also addressed to the fraternal Muslim states. The breaking up of the Arab people into different social classes (*ṭabaqāt*) of which some own a lot and others little is denounced.[26] A more equal distribution of the oil revenues among all Arab countries must be developed.[27] The less egoistic and more caring relations, which developed among Palestinians since the outbreak of the *Intifāḍa*, are praised as exemplary.

Thus we can distinguish a vague discourse of social justice and equality. It takes the form of a Third World discourse when dealing with the international order. At the same time, communist and socialist ideologies are completely discredited by the Islamists as man-made and secular programmes. One interesting aspect is the use of this discourse in the struggle against Israel. The conflict, supposedly based on religious ground, is attributed a social component. Evidence for a description of the Jews as attached to worldly affairs and possessions is found in the *Ḥadīth*-literature and biography of the Prophet. The wealth and well-being of the Israelis can furthermore indicate their condemnation in the Hereafter: God might have decided to leave them in a dazed state of wealth in order to maintain them in unbelief.[28] Nevertheless, the call for the struggle against Israel in the name of social justice does not seem to be mainly based on sacred Islamic scriptures. This line of argument is rather a direct reflection of the disastrous socio-economic situation in the Occupied Territories. The term "bourgeois" obviously does not refer to any concept or idea of Islamic origin. Thus I would argue that this is another example of the Islamists' capacity to respond to the need of their constituencies. The lack of economic progress and social advancement has been described as the driving force behind the *Intifāḍa*. Thus, social dissatisfaction is channelled into the struggle against the Israelis, who could easily have been perceived by the mass of Palestinian wage labourers also as employers and exploiters.

Nevertheless, the general social aspect of the Islamists' programme, which is probably one of its most attractive features, follows the classical line of modern fundamentalist thought. At the centre of the Muslim Brotherhood's activity, this aspect was thoroughly developed by its theoretician Sayyid Qutb in his book *Social Justice in Islam* (*Al-'Adāla al-Ijtimā'iyya fī l-Islām*). Qutb declares that social justice is inherent in Islam. Islam contains the basic principles of social justice by which he first understands the equality of men. Emanating from this principle, he considers Islam to guarantee the right of the poor to more wealth[29] as well as the constraints put on the power of Islamic administrators who derive their authority from the Muslim community. As their laws are derived from religious principles which state that all men are equal, any kind of oppression should be excluded.[30]

The main point of Qutb's explanation is the unity of worship/belief and practical life/behaviour. Faith is not only expressed in worship, but in all activities of life. The examples of the Qur'ān and the *Ḥadīths* quoted by Qutb are even designed to prove that faith expressed in practical work is more valuable than mere worship. The religious duty of Muslims to practice their faith in all social, legal, economic and other relationships[31] guarantees social justice in a "truly" Islamic society. *Ḥamās* follows Qutb in this thought, claiming that its "ideology" includes an Islamic understanding of all domains of life such as economy, politics, education, society, law, art and science.[32]

Qutb and the *Ḥamās*-activists both view Islam as a distinct historical totality that permeates and rules every domain of life.[33] Qutb admits that throughout Islamic history there have been rulers that oppressed the people in the name of Islam and persecuted those who thought differently, but he prevents further investigation by characterising these examples as "abnormal" for Islamic history.[34] Qutb does not seem to be aware of the relationship between ideology and power.[35] He does not realise that what he believes to be the "true" essence of Islam is just one possible interpretation, from the view of the "deprived masses".[36] *Ḥamās* follows Qutb closely in this point: there can only be one universal understanding of the Islamic message, the defense of the poor and weak; a deviating view cannot be accepted. On the other hand, the Islamists pay more attention to the question of power and ideology than their venerable predecessor because their struggle seems more clearly aimed at seizing or at least sharing political power. *Ḥamās* has a more refined technical vocabulary to analyse existing Arab regimes and their politics; the movement understands very well the impact of modern media. But when considering Islam, the dynamics of individual interests and power struggle seem to be forgotten and a monolithic view of Islam and its followers prevails.

NOTES

1. FM, April 1990, p. 5.
2. FM, May 1990, p. 39.
3. Ibid.
4. FM, January 1990, p. 20.
5. Ibid.
6. FM, May 1990, p. 35.
7. FM, September 1990, p. 13.
8. FM, June 1990, pp. 26–27.
9. Ibid.
10. Ibid.
11. Ibid.
12. FM, June 1990, p. 28.
13. *Mīthāq*, p. 35.
14. Qur'ān, Sura 99.
15. *Mīthāq*, p. 35.
16. FM, June 1990, p. 28.
17. Rudolph Peters in "Erneuerungsbewegungen", p. 95, makes the important point that fundamentalism is often falsely equated with conservatism. Conservatism is by definition the endeavour to consolidate the existing order and to oppose change. Fundamentalism clearly does not defend the existing order, which is perceived as deviating from the true principles of Islam. Its followers struggle for change and improvement of the existing social and political order.
18. Watt, *Islamic Fundamentalism and Modernity*, pp. 6–8 and pp. 8–14.
19. Qur'ān, 33:40.
20. Qur'ān, 3:110.

21. FM, May 1990, p. 45.
22. FM, January 1990, p. 15; FM, March 1990, p. 31; FM, November 1990, p. 42.
23. FM, January 1990, p. 8.
24. FM, April 1990, p. 35.
25. See Chapter Six of this volume. See also FM, September 1990, p. 6.
26. FM, September 1990, p. 4.
27. FM, September 1990, p. 6.
28. This idea is based on the Qur'ānic verse 9:85: "And let not their wealth and their children please you. God only desires to torment them thereby in this world, that their souls should depart while they are unbelievers."
29. Qutb, *Al-'Adāla al-Ijtimā'iyya fī l-Islām*, p. 19.
30. Ibid, pp. 16–17.
31. Ibid, p. 12.
32. *Mīthāq*, p. 7.
33. Ironically, Qutb joins in this perception with many Western orientalists and anthropologists who have to fight the reproach of essentialising.
34. By contrast, Muslim rulers deviating from the Islamic path are an omnipresent feature in the contemporary era.
35. This is all the more astonishing as he defines Islam as a body of general, universal and unchanging principles, leaving the application in detail to be determined by time and the specific problems that might arise (Quṭb, *Al-'Adāla al-Ijtimā'iyya fī l-Islām*, p. 19). This view implies that there is a variety of applications of one and the same universal principle. The next step would logically have been to investigate what might determine different applications which would have led to the question of interests and power.
36. He could also have stressed the Islamic rule that the community should obey its leader in order to avoid civil strife (*fitna*). This principle was generally emphasised by Islamic rulers in order to stabilise their position.

CHAPTER EIGHT

Inner Enemy: The Palestinian Liberation Organisation

Hamās is convinced that Islam corresponds to the "real nature" of the Palestinians and consequently a solution to the Palestinian problem has to be Islamic and achieved by means based on Islamic beliefs. Together with this conviction goes the call for a democratisation of political life. This call was mainly made in connection with a harsh criticism of the existing Arab regimes, but it also applied to the situation in the Occupied Territories.[1]

Ḥamās questioned the Palestinian Liberation Organisation's claim to be the sole representative of the Palestinian people. This had become necessary as the PLO succeeded to strengthen its role as representative of the Palestininas by proclaiming the independence of Palestine at the 19th. Palestinian National Congress 1988 in Algiers. This implicit recognition of the existence of Israel was interpreted as a proof of pragmatism and consolidated the position of the PLO in the international arena. This constituted a serious challenge to the political movements inside the Occupied Territories. The *Mīthāq* was probably elaborated as a response to this development questioning the PLO's right to speak for the Palestinians. *Ḥamās* stressed the ideological and programmatic differences between the two organisations and claimed to be closer to the will of the Palestinians, a will clearly expressed in the *Intifāḍa*.

Departing from Muslim Brotherhood practices in Egypt, *Ḥamās* acts as a political movement – even though it formally denies being a mere political party.[2] Underlying its attack on the representative role of the PLO is the conviction that *Ḥāmās* and other groups following an Islamic programme are truly "centrist" (*wasaṭī*) movements.[3] The Islamic ideology can neither be labelled as left nor right; it is neutral between East and West and contains no extremist positions.[4] It is thus "balanced" (*mu'tadil*) and "independent" (*mustaqill*) and is therefore considered more representative than any political party based on a different programme. The idea of the Islamic *Umma* as a "community of the middle way" (*Umma wasaṭ*) goes back to the Qur'ān.[5] Mawdudi explains the meaning of this verse as designating a "distinguished group of people which follows the path of justice and equity, of balance and moderation, a group which occupies a central position among the nations of the world so that its friendship with all is based on righteousness and justice and none receives its support in wrong and injustice".[6] This special position invests the community at the same time "with the leadership of all mankind".[7] In a simple transfer, the political movement *Ḥamās* appropriated for itself these Qur'ānic qualifications of the *Umma*. We can assume from these basic convictions that *Ḥamās* believed in its right to leadership of the Palestinians, but in the open political discussion the movement presented itself as more modest and calls for a multi-party-system. The reasons for this restraint were probably the realistic evaluation of the strength of *Fataḥ* and the PLO in the Territories and the recognition of the specific needs in a pre-national situation of an occupied country.

This peaceful coexistence with the PLO despite different views found its expression in the *Mīthāq* where the relation between the PLO and *Ḥamās* was characterized as the one of a father to a son, the relation between brothers, relatives or friends.[8] *Ḥamās* stressed that both organisations are linked by having the same "homeland", "fate" and "calamity" (*waṭanuna wāḥid, muṣābuna wāḥid, maṣīruna wāḥid*).[9]

But this closeness could not blurr the fundamental differences between *Ḥamās* and the PLO. Responding to a call to participate in the Palestinian National Congress, the Islamic Restistance Movement explained that true unity between *Ḥamās* and the PLO could only exist if there were agreement on the following essential points: who is the enemy, what is the goal and by which means do we hope to achieve it?[10] In 1990 there was only agreement on the first of these points: Zionism/ Judaism in the form of the Israeli state is the common enemy. There cannot not be unity between *Ḥamās* and the PLO as long as the PLO sticks to its secular orientation laid down in the National Charter and as long as it makes concessions on the issues of territory and rights of the Palestinians.[11] As long as the PLO holds on to these positions, *Ḥamās* cannot participate and take over responsibility for a policy based on it.[12]

For a collaboration in the PNC after an eventual adjustment of the National Charter, *Ḥamās* required certain conditions to be fulfilled. According to the "Islamic way", PNC members should be elected and not appointed, districts should be represented according to population. If there were no elections, then representations "should match the strength of the forces on the ground" and for political, financial and administrative reasons the number of members of the PNC should be reduced and as its role limited.[13] In June 1990 *Ḥamās* claimed at least 40 to 50 percent of the PNC-seats for itself.[14] The *Ḥamās*-leader Jamal Hamami expressed his regret that *Ḥamās* cannot participate in the work of the PNC which would be "necessary and right", as the voice of Islam should be heard in the Palestinian parliament.[15]

Still *Ḥamās* emphasised its firm conviction that all fights have to be avoided, thinking especially about PLO attacks on the Islamists and the oppression of Islamic activists in Israeli prison by PLO members.[16] "The door remains open and the hand stretched out in order to collaborate with all Palestinian forces no matter what their system of thought is".[17] *Ḥamās* contributed to this unity for example by not answering treacherous attacks launched against them by the PLO through its organ *Filasṭīn al-Thawra*.[18]

Ḥamās tried to ideologically consolidate its position as an independent political movement by quoting a slogan used by the *Fataḥ* in the 1970s saying that "criticism does not mean necessarily fragmentation of the strength".[19] It pointed to the period between 1964 and 1967 when there existed several organisations outside the PLO because there was no agreement about the path of the revolution.[20] "True national unity" (*waḥda waṭaniyya ḥaqīqiyya*), based on the agreement on the three points mentioned above, thus only existed between 1967 and 1974, ending when the 12th PNC adopted a ten-point-plan[21] accepting the idea of the establishment of an independent state on parts of the Palestinian territory only. The other justification for *Ḥamās'* choice to struggle separately from the PLO despite the need for unity invoked frequently by the movement itself was the model of the Western state. The movement affirmed that opposition to the government or the refusal to participate in the parliament do not signify that you put yourself outside the state and legal framework.[22]

Thirsty for power, the PLO was seen as wanting to rally all Palestinians behind it in order to allow the organisation to speak in the name of the entire population. Thus political manoeuvres were at the base of the offer for *Ḥamās* to participate in the PNC which was only made after the PLO could not ignore the Islamic forces any more.[23] As *Ḥamās* did not accept this game, the PLO again launched attacks against it. The Islamists even suggested that the PLO was ready to make any concession to the USA and Israel in order to get a solution "before fundamentalism (*uṣūlīyya*) and extremism (*taṭarruf*) will control the region".[24]

Without giving any proof, *Ḥamās* claimed that the Palestinian organisations outside the PLO were as strong and had as many members as the PLO itself – which constituted evidence for the existence of different opinions among the Palestinian people.[25] But the Islamists went even further, asserting again and again that they represented the will of the people, invoking the success of the Islamic groups in the elections in Jordan or in universities in the Occupied Territories. They asserted that the gap between the PLO and the rest of the Palestinian people was growing. While the PLO called for an agreement that only serves the Zionist aims, the population refused any fragmentation or concession of their legal rights.[26] After the failure of the PLO peace-initiative in which it "sacrified everything without gaining anything",[27] the Palestinians knew that the PLO had nothing more to offer the USA and its "foster son" (*rabīb*)[28] than to dissolve itself. The "Zionist entity" would at best agree on the right to self-determination for the Palestinians.[29]

Filasṭīn al-Muslima published the whole of a lecture given in Amman by a professor of political science in Bir-Zeit University, Ziad Abu-Amr, whose research confirmed the claims that *Ḥamās* better represented the Palestinian people than the PLO did.[30] He talked of a "void of PLO leadership" inside the Territories due to the occupation policy of systematic expulsion and arrests of leading figures and cadres, but also due to the failure of the PLO leadership outside the Territories over the last twenty years to build up a serious sub-structure inside the Territories. This evolution led to the appearance of a leadership inside the Territories which seemed to have no experience and thus allowed a growing interference in the *Intifāḍa* of the PLO leadership from the outside. But this PLO leadership was not in harmony with the reality in the Territories. Abu-Amr stated that popular committees exercised power without referring back to any ultimate hierarchical instance. This confirmed *Ḥamās*' view of the "Islamic" *Intifāḍa* as a democratic, popular movement expressing the will of the people. Carried by this movement, *Ḥamās* graciously offered the PLO the chance to rejoin the "*Jihād* of the stone-throwing children" as well as the leadership of the *Intifāḍa* after having recognised its failure and reconsidered its position.[31]

At this point, the constant reference to Sheikh Qassam shows its full implications. The *Mīthāq* mentions Sheikh Izz al-Din al-Qassam as one of the predecessors of the *Ḥamās*-movement[32] and the journal *Filasṭīn al-Muslima* portrays him regularly as a model by publishing articles on his life and deeds. As Nels Johnson points out in his excellent book *Islam and the Politics of Meaning in Palestinian Nationalism*, the movement of Sheikh Qassam marked a "turning point in the nature of Palestinian politics";[33] populist Islam replaced the moderate opposition of the traditional Palestinian elite, mainly notables, in the struggle against Zionists and British mandate power. Factionalism and moderation had eroded the position of the traditional elite, which was already felt in the riots of 1929.[34] In the Qassam-movement just prior to the 1935 revolt, the masses were acting for the first time on their own without the direction of the traditional elite.[35] Johnson judges this movement as the "first phase of a transition from elite to mass political action".[36] Sheikh Qassam used Islamic concepts in order to make the people participate in social and political action; his ideology thus represents a classical example of "Islamic populism".[37] Qassam's legacy to Palestinian political culture is in Johnson's view a "broadened and heightened popular conception of resistance as a religious, and therefore a moral and ethical duty".[38]

This is exactly where *Ḥamās*' appeal laid. Its followers no longer felt represented by the PLO leadership whose members lived outside the Territories, were in general well-educated, relatively wealthy and who moderated their position in 1988 while the oppression in the Territories increased daily. The socio-economic and ideological gap became too large. Under the direction of *Ḥamās*, differentiating itself from the PLO by the use of religious rhetoric, the people in the Territories acted on their own, independently from the traditional political elite. The constant reference to Sheikh Qassam as a model and guide for their struggle thus again confirmed that *Ḥamās* was fighting a struggle over political power and leadership – despite its altruistic rhetoric and the repeated denial of any self-interest.

How else can one explain its violent and public reaction to a PLO text using an apparently Qur'ānic quote in its heading – which in fact turned out to be neither a Qur'ānic verse nor a *Ḥadīth*, but merely a saying amongst certain righteous Muslims?[39] The first part of the text, written by Yassir Arafat and originally published in *Filasṭīn al-Thawra* in January 1990, was published under the title "To whom it may concern" together with the rectifications. The Islamic message and tradition is considered the exclusive domain and political programme of *Ḥamās* – the other Islamist groups being of negligible significance – and beware the one who tries his hand at it.

What about the other organisations and parties of the Palestinian political scene? They are all under control. The other Islamic groups are linked to *Ḥamās* through their common reliance on God. There is no doubt as to the solidarity among those who fight to realise the directives of the "Book" and the "Sunna".[40] The Qur'ānic verse quoted in support fits perfectly: "And hold fast God's cord altogether and do not scatter (...)."[41] As Mawdudi explains, this refers to the state of the Arabs on the eve of the advent of Islam when animosities among tribes regularly broke out into fighting.[42] Here we have another striking example of how the emphasis in the Qur'ān on group identity and solidarity, delimiting Muslims from outside enemies, facilitates the use of the Qur'ān in contemporary conflicts. According to its conviction that there is only one version of Islam, the Islamic Resistance Movement goes further, asserting that everybody who wants an Islamic state in Palestine is (automatically) part of *Ḥamās* and its effort.[43] The unknown authors who issued faked statements in the name of *Ḥamās* are virulently attacked and *Ḥamās* is presented as the original Islamic movement.[44]

There remain the communist groups whose fate is sealed anyway. The failure of communism in the Eastern European countries is interpreted as a confirmation of the Islamic world-view.[45] Sayyid Qutb predicted this failure twenty years ago, based on his knowledge of Islam.[46] The Western communists today recognise the failure of their ideology themselves; only the Arab communists refuse to do so.[47] But the masses already chose their programme for change[48] which is the Islamic one. More than one former communist activist was convinced by the exemplary behaviour of Islamist co-inmates in Israeli prisons to join the ranks of the Islamic Resistance Movement.[49]

In this phase of Palestinian politics, since the outbreak of the Intifada in December 1987 until the beginning of the peace-negociations and finally the Declaration of Principles (DOP) in September 1993 which fundamentally changes the political landscape, *Ḥamās* has been emerging as a political force. In the *Mīthāq* in August 1988 positioned itself modestly as the "son" or "brother" of the PLO and underlined the common goals and aspirations of both organisations. But departing from the prior attitude to ignore the PLO and to build up parallel institutions, it slowly began to establish itself as a competitor to the PLO that pretends to be the sole representative of the Palestinians. *Ḥamās* sketches out an ideological alternative to the PLO's new moderate position by defending with religious arguments the uncompromising attitude taken up by the PLO for so long. It rejects the PLO's secular vision of statehood and opposes it with a nationalist ideology supposedly based on traditional Islam. Despite the eagerness of *Ḥamās* to be recognised as an alternative force with an alternative political programme, the criticism of the PLO and Arafat is still restrained and moderate. The tone will change when Arafat seriously becomes engaged in peace-discussion and when he finally strengthens his movement at the expense of the Islamists by signing the peace accords.

NOTES

1. I want to remind the reader that the material used in this section dates from 1988 to 1991, the first years of the Intifada, when *Ḥamās* started to challenge the PLO. In Chapter eighteen I will analyse the *Ḥamās*' attitude towards the Palestinian National Authority (PNA) created on the basis of the Oslo Peace Accords.
2. FM , September 1990, p. 8.
3. FM, April 1990, p. 25.

4. Ibid.
5. Qur'ān, 2:143: "Thus We have made you a midmost nation (...)."
6. Mawdudi, *Tafhīm*, Vol. I, p. 121.
7. Ibid.
8. *Mīthāq*, p. 27.
9. Ibid.
10. FM, July 1990, p. 25.
11. FM, July 1990, p. 14. This refers the recognition of the existence of Israel and the acceptance of a two-state-solution by the PLO in 1988.
12. Ibid.
13. FM, May 1990, p. 13.
14. FM, June 1990, p. 10. It is not known on which basis *Ḥamās* claims these percentages.
15. FM, June 1990, p. 10.
16. FM, July 1990, p. 14.
17. Ibid.
18. FM, August 1990, pp. 10–11.
19. FM, July 1990, p. 25.
20. Ibid. *Filasṭīn al-Muslima* underlines that Fataḥ only entered the PLO after their programme was amended in their sense. FM, July 1990, p. 25.
21. FM, July 1990,p. 25. For the text of the plan, issued on 9th of June 1974 in Cairo, see Xavier Baron, *Les Palestiniens. Un Peuple*, (Paris, 1984), p. 519.
22. FM, September 1990, p. 14.
23. FM, July 1990, p. 14.
24. FM, April 1990, p. 3.
25. FM, July 1990, p. 26.
26. FM, January, 1990, p. 3.
27. FM, June 1990, p. 2.
28. FM, January 1990, p. 3.
29. Ibid.
30. FM, January 1990, p. 26.
31. FM, April 1990, p. 3.
32. *Mīthāq*, p. 10.
33. Nels Johnson, *Islam and the Politics of Meaning in Palestinian Nationalism*, (London, 1982), p. 31.
34. Ibid, p. 36.
35. Ibid.
36. Ibid, p. 47.
37. Ibid, p. 54.
38. Ibid, p. 58.
39. FM, March 1990, p. 15.
40. *Mīthāq*, p. 25.
41. Qur'ān, 3:103.
42. Mawdudi, op. cit., Vol. I, p. 276.
43. FM, September 1990, p. 8.
44. Ibid.
45. FM, April 1990, p. 27.

46. Ibid.
47. FM, March 1990, p. 46.
48. Ibid.
49. FM, March 1990, p. 10.

CHAPTER NINE

Equality? The Christian Minority

The Islamists' view of religious minorities is crucial for the understanding of the principles underlying their ideas about democracy and the state. *Ḥamās'* position relies closely on the classical Islamic teaching on this question. There, Jews and Christians – as well as other non-Muslims possessing a scripture – are recognised as "People of the Book". Those residing in territory ruled by Muslims (*dār al-ḥarb*) were tolerated religious minorities, called *dhimmīs*. *Dhimma* means a contract which the believer agrees to respect and the violation of which makes him liable to blame (*dhamm*).[1] The security of life and property and an indefinite assurance of protection (*amān*) are guaranteed by the Muslim state.[2] But as *dhimmīs* are not true believers, they are not entitled to full membership in the Muslim brotherhood.[3] As a sign of submission to the Islamic state, *dhimmīs* have to pay a poll tax.[4]

Dhimmīs are only aggressed if they threaten or harm the Islamic *Umma*, which is exactly what the Jews living in Israel are seen to be doing. The Islamists emphasise that this is not at all the case with the Christians. "The growing Islamic current in Palestine does not threaten the Christians" is the title of a long article in *Filasṭīn al-Muslima* on the relations with the Christian minority among the Palestinians.[5]

The magazine points out that the Christian Palestinians suffer the same "Zionist" oppression and flee the same devastating economical and political conditions of life in the Territories as their Muslim fellows.[6] In contrast, Christians in Islamic societies are recognised as a "protected minority" and are never treated as "citizens of second, third or fourth class".[7] This tolerance stands in contrast to the Christian behaviour after the reconquista of Andalusia when they persecuted the

Muslims and destroyed all traces of them.[8] *Ḥamās* claims to be the movement of "all Palestinians, Muslims and Christians alike", and suggests that they were among the first to criticise the Zionist attacks on a building of the Orthodox church.[9] In a statement *Ḥamās* explicitly thanked the heads of the Christian churches for their condolence after the Temple Mount massacre.[10] Never are unjust acts said to have occurred against the Palestinian Christians, "except attacks against bars and wine-shops and similar institutions".[11] Responding to the fear expressed by the Pope about the future of the Christians in a Palestinian Islamic state, the Islamists argue that a state with a majority Muslim population should be ruled by Muslims.[12] The minority has to accept the view of the majority, this is the most basic democratic rule (*absaṭ al-a'rāf al-dīmuqrāṭiyya*).[13] They ask polemically what the Pope would say if the one and a half million Muslims living in Germany would impose their rule on the mainly Christian population of the country?[14]

The assertion of tolerance towards Christians laid down in the Qur'ān seems to match the interests of the moment. Only a united Palestinian population can stand up successfully against the united "Zionist enemy". Thus the Christians, who represent about five percent of the Palestinian population, have to be reassured and integrated in order to make them fight along with the Muslims against Israel. The Christians are promised equality with their fellow citizens in the future Palestinian state. But the classical Islamic theory about *dhimmīs* excludes the modern nation-state idea of equality of all citizens. *Dhimmīs* are not dealt with by Muslim governments as individual citizens or subjects of the state, but as members of a distinct and separate community.[15] Their status, rights and duties are exclusively derived from their membership of a protected minority. The concept of toleration separates religious minorities automatically from the Muslim political body. The religious duty of Muslims to establish an Islamic society on earth according to God's plan means that Muslims have to be installed in power. As P. J. Vatikiotis suggests, Muslims can share economic goods, social benefits and space with non-Muslim populations, but not power.[16] The Divine Order is considered to be the perfect just order – for Muslims and *dhimmīs* alike. Thus the religious character of the Muslim's venture on earth excludes the share of power with non-Muslims.

This classical Islamic view of protected religious minorities is incompatible with the Western idea of pluralism and equality of individual citizens in a nation-state. Christians and Jews are in fact different citizens than their Muslim fellow-men. It becomes obvious that the Islamists' idea of democracy and political pluralism is very different from the Western one. An ideological order that separates non-Muslims from the body politic by tolerating them, rejects the idea of political pluralism; it only allows political separation. The Islamists' claims that every group of a people must have the right to express its views openly[17] is limited by the conviction that non-Muslims have to recognise the superiority of Islam. No behaviour or statement impinging upon Islamic belief can be tolerated. The best proof for this is the Islamists' proclaimed right to close Christian bars and shops selling wine.[18] This is against Islamic law and thus is not subject to tolerance.

Furthermore this section provides another fine example of the intrusion of Western ideas into the traditional Islamic framework of thought. The Qur'ānic regulations on the subject of religious minorities are not sufficient as explanation. It would be desirable for them to satisfy Western standards. The acceptance of the superiority of Islam, which the Islamic doctrine demands from religious minorities, supposedly corresponds to the Western idea of political pluralism, which states that the minority accepts the decision of the majority. The explanation based on Islamic teaching has to satisfy the Western yardstick as well. The compatibility of Islamic and modern liberal thought has to be shown. Thus we detect here another example of the apologetic aspects of modern Islamic thought.

NOTES

1. Khadduri, op. cit., p. 176.
2. Ibid, p. 177.
3. Ibid.
4. Qur'ān, 9:29: "Fight those who do not believe in God (...) until they pay tribute out of hand and they are yielding."
5. FM, September 1990, p. 10.
6. Ibid, p. 11.
7. Ibid.
8. Ibid.
9. Ibid.

10. *Bayān Ḥamās* no. 65, 11.10.1990, in: FM, November 1990, p. 7.
11. Ibid, p. 11.
12. Ibid.
13. Ibid.
14. Ibid.
15. Vatikiotis, op. cit., p. 87.
16. Ibid, p. 55.
17. FM, July 1990, p. 25.
18. FM, September 1990, p. 11.

Chapter Ten

Ambiguity: Attitude towards the West

The West is perceived as genuinely hostile towards Islam and the Muslim countries. As I have mentioned previously, "the West" comprises the capitalist industrial nations as well as the former socialist countries of Eastern Europe. United in their common aim to harm Islam, they are considered by the Islamists as enemies of the *Umma*. Any strengthening of Islam represents a victory against the West. Thus every development or event in the Arab world is interpreted as reaction to the West. Furthermore, the Islamists' attitude towards the West and its institutions is ambiguous in a similiar way as their view of the Zionists and the state of Israel, where hatred mixes with admiration.

Reporting the victory of the Islamic Salvation Front in the elections in Algeria, *Filasṭīn al-Muslima* emphasised the anxiety aroused in the French government.[1] This was even mentioned in the title of the story, showing the importance accorded to the reaction of the Western country. The reactions of various French politicians to the Islamist's victory were quoted at length. The Islamists stressed that the former minister of foreign affairs, Michel Jobert, even threatened the newly elected forces by saying that the army had not yet said its last word in this affair;[2] only to state in the end that France held no more power over Algeria.

These reactions lead the Islamists to blame the French for "betraying the supreme principles of the French Revolution which are *liberté, égalité* and *fraternité*".[3] The French were accused of not according the right to democracy and to a multi-party-system to their former colonies and protectorates.[4] They were seen as wanting to limit these achievements, "which they consider European",[5] to Europe and trying to withhold them from the "poor countries" in the world in order to prolong their dominiation over them.[6] While the West encouraged the spread of democracy in Eastern Europe, it opposed a similar development in the Islamic world.[7] The Islamists equated this behaviour with "racism".[8] The changing Western attitude towards the evolution of the same system in different places was described as "schizophrenic" (*shīzūfrīniyya*).[9] The West was only afraid of Islam because it did not know that it is in fact the basis of Western civilization.[10]

The Islamists thus clearly accept the principles of the French Revolution, they only question their European origin. This further illustrates the Islamists' capacity to absorb through Islamisation. In order to avoid admiration for a non-Islamic achievement, they transform the whole Western civilisation into a mere prolongation of Islamic civilisation. This process allows them to defend certain principles of Western origin, thus securing them the support of the West; at the same time, the indigenous population can accept them easily as well because they seem to stand firmly on Islamic ground.

Another domain in which the Islamist's ambiguous feelings towards the West prevail, is the field of the media. On one hand, the Islamists state that the Western press defends the interests of the West: first they were silent about the question of Jewish mass emmigration from the Soviet Union in order not to raise protest from the Arab world. Once this goal was achieved, they talked about it at length, this time intending to make the Muslims despair and to make them accept any conditions for a settlement of the Palestinian question.[11]

On the other hand, Western media are considered much more reliable than any Arab press organ. Thus the Western press "generally puts the *Intifāḍa* in the right light"[12] and "recognised the importance of Islam" in the contemporary Arab world.[13] Thus *Filasṭīn al-Muslima* even published a translation of an article on the Islamists written by the British journalist Patrick Seal.[14] The Arab press, in contrast, defamed the Islamists or suppressed information about them.[15] On the issue of opposition against the Arab regimes, the Islamists used the Western press to got more accurate information than they get from the countries concerned. Thus they based their criticism of the Marrocan official reaction to demonstrations of opposition in the streets on information spread by Western media.[16] They did not believe the statements issued by the Marrocan ruler.[17] In their attitude towards the Western media, the Islamists were obviously inconsistent. Unlike their way of dealing with the Western values of democracy and freedom, they did not make any attempt to justify their extensive use of Western media on any Islamic ground.

The terminology used for dealing with the West is interesting; we find old hats like "imperialism" and "neo-colonialism", but we also see the United States referred to as "Cowboy", "Remote Control" and "Rambo" (*rāmbū*).[18] This terminology is revealing in two ways. It shows that popular culture in the Arab-Muslim world is impregnated by Western "cultural" symbols; the international mass media culture reaches the most aloof Egyptian village. Coca Cola and Dallas became part of everyday life in most parts of the world.[19] Thus it becomes more and more difficult to draw a straight line between Islamic and Western culture. The terminology also reveals what aspects of Western culture are the most widespread among other peoples: free sex, intrigue, corruption, violence. For many less educated people, the West signifies degeneration, the loosening of morals and the loss of values. This could explain why the fundamentalist movement is successful in presenting the West as evil and presenting allegedly Islamic traditions as superior.

NOTES

1. FM, July 1990, p. 10.
2. Ibid.
3. Ibid.
4. Ibid.
5. Ibid.
6. Ibid.
7. FM, May 1990, p. 46.
8. FM, July 1990, p. 10.
9. FM, March 1990, p. 11.
10. Ibid, p. 10.
11. FM, March 1990, p. 2.
12. FM, April 1990, p. 15.
13. FM, March 1990, p. 38.
14. FM, June 1990, p. 1.
15. FM, April 1990, p. 15.

16. FM, June 1990, p. 6.
17. Ibid.
18. FM, September 1990, p. 4.
19. See Sami Zubaida, "The Nation State in the Middle East", p. 161, in: Zubaida, *Islam, the People and the State*.

PART TWO

Application of General World View to Specific Political Events

CHAPTER ELEVEN

The Gulf-War 1990/91

On the 2 August 1990, Iraq invaded her neighbour Kuwait and took control of the capital and the oil fields. This was a complete surprise even though there had been tensions for some time between the two governments.[1] The UN Security Council and the Arab League both condemned the invasion and called for an immediate withdrawl. The PLO abstained from the vote.[2] The Arab League also condemned any foreign intervention, but nevertheless failed to form a joint Arab force to stand against Iraq. The inter-Arab differences grew stronger so that the emergency Arab summit which convened in Cairo on the 10 August fell through: Saddam Hussein had formally annexed Kuwait to Iraq on the 8 August just after US President George Bush had despatched the first American soldiers to Saudi-Arabia in order to defend the Kingdom against any Iraqi attack. The prospect of a US military presence on Arab territory shifted the debate from the issue of the Iraqi invasion to the issue of Western neocolonialism. On the 12 August, Saddam Hussein suggested the famous "linkage" saying that he would withdraw from Kuwait if Israel withdrew from the Occupied Territories and Syria ended its occupation of Lebanon. On the 16 January 1991, the Western-Arab-Alliance[3] launched a massive air campaign against Iraq and thus started the second Gulf War during which several Iraqi Scud missiles hit Israel. An allied ground attack launched on the 23 February led to the liberation of Kuwait which was officially announced on the 27 February.

The stationing of American and European troops in Saudi-Arabia and the following military fight against the Iraqi army brought the Arab world into their closest contact with the ominous "West" since colonial times. The broad public in most Arab countries sided with Iraq, thus contrasting in the most obvious way with their governments' positions. For the Islamists in all Arab states, especially those in Palestine, the Gulf-War was a great moment because it seemed to confirm their world view in an impressive manner; and those views were shared in an unprecedented way by the majority of the Arab population. In fact, the reaction of the population often pushed the Islamists to a more open position of support for Saddam Hussein than they had wished to take with regards to their main financiers, the Gulf-states and Saudi-Arabia.[4] Nevertheless, the Western military intervention gave the Islamists the chance to become – for a short time – the leaders of the masses against their "corrupt" governments to an extent which they only had dreamt about until then.

In Palestine, the PLO and *Ḥamās* were facing the same ideological dilemma: should they follow the popular sentiment in favour of Saddam Hussein, the fearless contender of the West and the "Zionist" state, or should they distance themselves from the occupier of Kuwait, which is one of their financial benefactors?[5] But as the PLO sided quickly with Iraq[6], *Ḥamās* could not simply play the popular card against a leadership ignoring the will of the people. Jean-Francois Legrain believes that the decision of the PLO to side with Saddam Hussein played an important role in the calculations of the Islamic movement's leadership to "quietly choose to restrain its natural enthusiasm for any anti-Western agent and in anticipation that the Iraqi 'liberator of Palestine' would fail".[7] The fundamentalist writing in *Filasṭīn al Muslima* does not confirm this view. It is true that it took *Ḥamās* two weeks to publish its position on the Iraqi invasion of Kuwait[8]. It certainly is interesting that the Islamic Resistance Movement called for 19 days of strikes between 3 August 1990 and 9 January 1991, but that only two of these actions were in protest against the Iraqi invasion. This silence nevertheless seems to express much more the hesitation of the *Ḥamās* leadership when confronted with this complex situation than the clear decision not to alienate Kuwait and the other Gulf-sponsors. The Islamic Resistance Movement did not hesitate to virulently attack the Arab members of the military alliance, namely the Egyptian, Syrian and Saudi govenments and the Kuwaitis. The organisation clearly stated that it "sides with Iraq" in the hostilities.[9]

The fundamentalists repeated on several occasions that they opposed the Iraqi invasion of Kuwait. "We know and even believe that the Iraqi decision to invade Kuwait was a false step."[10] "The Islamic world in general considered the Iraqi aggression of Kuwait as a mistake."[11] "But the agreement on this view makes many people blind for the right analysis."[12] *Ḥamās* insisted on an "Islamic Arabic peaceful solution".[13] *Filasṭīn al-Muslima* rejected the view that any inter-Arab solution was "only idle talk" (*mugarrad hurā*).[14] Those who pretended this and would "laugh about it" were the Arab regimes that called immediately for foreign troops to solve the crisis and thereby prevented any Arab diplomatic solution.[15] The Gulf-states did not pay attention to the efforts to prevent a war and "even cooperated with the US to make the Rabat summit fail that King Hussein II had called for (...)".[16] Furthermore, the Western and Arab states of the alliance against Iraq would use "terrorist methods to frighten states and populations in order to make them give up the position that called for a diplomatic solution to the crisis."[17]

Those who claimed that only a foreign military force could make Iraq retreat from Kuwait "simplify the problem in a naive way" and in fact did not wish any other solution.[18] Those states shied away from the energy-consuming effort to find an inter-Arab solution. "They put their eggs in the American basket and fall asleep, waiting that the US come to terms with Iraq and its army (...)".[19]

Thus, in the Islamists' eyes, there was no doubt that an Arab diplomatic solution was impeded upon by the West and their regional allies. In this respect, there was no distinction made between the Western powers and the Arab Muslim governments. The Arab regimes participating in the alliance were accused in the most open manner of having undermined a negotiated solution. The Islamists even went so far as to hold the Gulf states responsible for the outbreak of the actual warfare. However, it is true that this line of analysis and criticism emanated much more clearly from the writing in the *Ḥamās* mouth piece *Filasṭīn al-Muslima* than from the communiqués of *Ḥamās* distributed in the Occupied Territories.

A long article was dedicated to the development of the attitude of people and leaders in the Maghreb which can be considered representative for gradual opinion-making in most Arab states.[20] The

Maghreb governments opposed the Iraqi invasion of Kuwait and consequently supported the Kuwaitis in their demands for withdrawl and asked for an Arab solution. But the "call for help" (*instinjād*) from American and Western forces "made friends and other close people turn away" from the Kuwaitis, because at that point the slogan of the "liberation of Kuwait'" was used as a pretext to create an "insolent military force in the Gulf with the United States at its head." The "scale of the balance" (*al-kiffa*) began to bend against the Gulf states because of their preparation for war instead of looking for a peaceful solution.

The link made between the Iraqi-Kuwaiti conflict and the Palestine question established by Saddam Hussein and the rapid internationalisation of the conflict made it easy for the Islamists to analyse the events within their general world view. The Christian and Jewish West was fighting every Muslim country that was becoming strong and able to threaten the domination of the West – in this case Iraq; and at the heart of this world-wide struggle was the Israeli-Palestinian conflict as a "sort of microcosm to the larger predicament".[21]

The Islamists described the military engagement of the US as yet another aggression of the West against the Islamic *Umma*, another expression of the eternal religious conflict. Thus the United States were said to have launched the "eighth crusade against the Muslims".[22] *Ḥamās* describes the Western troops as "forces of infidelity" (*quwwāt al-kufr*) and "unbelievers" (*al-kuffār*).[23] Another time they spoke of the "Christian mischievous aggression against our religion".[24] Those army forces did not enter any Arab Muslim country, except Saudi-Arabia, which houses the two most holy Muslim places, Mekka and Medina. To emphasise the religious character of the events *Filasṭīn al-Muslima* often used the expression "the soil of the two holy places" (*arḍ al-ḥaramayn*)[25] to design the Wahhabite Kingdom. Iraq was thus leading a battle against "the historical enemies of the *Umma*".[26] Those enemies were various, some rather ancient, others of a more contemporary nature. The US-forces entering Saudi-Arabia were called "Nazi-forces"[27] and the subsequent war against Iraq was described as the "worst imperialistic, Zionist attack in human history".[28]

Again and again, the Islamists stated that the Western intervention was directed against the Muslim people and not against one political leader who did wrong. As a proof of this theory, they mentioned that the military and economic boycott, imposed by the "so-called security council", was sufficient to realise the two pretended aims of the US intervention: the withdrawl of Iraq from Kuwait and the destruction of the Iraqi military power.[29] *Ḥamās* deplored the undifferentiated bombing of military and civilian targets that proved the "extent of the Western hatred of Islam and the Muslims" (*madā ḥaqdihim 'alā al-Islām*).[30] This "ideological concept" (*tassawwur 'aqā' idī*) was said to link the West and the Jews more than just economic and security interests.[31] According to *Ḥamās*, one of the true goals of the Western invasion was the "establishment of the 'Greater Israel'" as laid down in the texts of the Talmud.[32] The invasion of Iraq should "facilitate Israel to conquer Jordan" (*ghazw al-'urdun*).[33]

This is another clear application of *Ḥamās*' world view and its internal inconsistencies. The West, characterised through its support of "Zionism" and the Jewish influence on its thought and politics, was waging a new war against Islam, a direct continuation of the medieval crusades and modern Imperialism and colonialism. As shown previously, the "Zionists" are believed to dream of the extension of their rule "from the Nile to the Euphrates" in order to dominate the whole region.[34] The presumption that Israeli interests guided Western intervention in the Gulf allowed the Islamists to portray the conflict as a new chapter of the historical story of the Jewish opposition to the Prophet Muhammad in the 7th century as transmitted in the Qur'ān and the *Ḥadīth*. The allies of the Jews were the Western powers – symbolised by the US – who were seen to be strongly influenced by Jews who were even held responsible for the harmful Western influences within Muslim societies. Thus, the ancient pattern fits the present very well, whereas the naming of the Western forces as "Nazi forces" is out of any context and meaningless. It was probably used simply as a synonym for outstanding brutality and cruelty – as when they speak about "Jewish Nazism" as we have seen before. This use of the term "Nazi" implies an extraordinary lack of historical consciousness, a fact that would at least confirm the selective and sometimes arbitrary use of history by the Islamists.

The establishment of the "Greater Israel" was seen only as a microcosm of a larger Western-Jewish master-plan. The ultimate goal, according to *Ḥamās*, was the destruction of the military, economic, cultural and developing forces in order to prevent the *Umma* from regaining its glory (*isti'ādat majdihā*) and building its own civilisation (*binā' ḥaḍāratiha*) by ending the dependency (*taba'īya*) and the injustice (*ẓulm*).[35] These themes had no particular Islamic or religious character; they have long been part of secular nationalism, Pan-Arabism and Arab socialism. Thus, the analysis of the true aims of the foreign intervention appealed to large layers of the Arab Muslim population, to Islamists as well as to their worst opponents. A famous Arab feminist was quoted to have defended her decision to side with Iraq on British television by saying that the Arabs have the right to have their own dictators if they want to.[36]

The fundamentalists were conviced that the fight against their own corrupt regimes was intrinsically linked to the historical struggle with the West. The latter can only be won if the Muslims take their affairs out of their governments' hands and into their own. The United States was said to have waited for an occasion to intervene directly in the Middle East because it felt that the region had been "slipping out of its control" for several years.[37] The credit was entirely to the "true" Muslim people who were gradually turning away from those among their leaders who were deferential to the West. This further illustrates the important differentiation that the Islamists make between the true Muslim people and their corrupt, deviant leaders; a beloved and frequently repeated assertion that was clearly proven in this conflict, especially in the case of Egyptian President Hosni Mubarak who joined the Western-Gulf-alliance against Iraq while the Egyptians showed their support for their Iraqi brothers in huge street demonstrations. In Syria, the other Arab non-Gulf state to take a position against Iraq, the divergence was said to be the same, except that in the merciless dictatorial system under President Hafez al-Asad there was no possibility of the people manifesting its will.[38] "With their heart all Syrians are with Iraq", said the journal.[39] The Asad-regime was conscious of the popular feeling, and so brought back part of its troops from Lebanon to guarantee domestic order.[40]

Mubarak and Asad were called the "representatives of the United States" in the region (*wukalā' amrīkā fī l-minṭaqa*)[41] that used this crisis in a "dirty way" disregarding the "wellbeing of the *Umma* (*maṣlaḥa lī l-Umma*)".[42] The Egyptian regime was described as the "executive hand" of the US (*yaduhu al-munaffidha*).[43] But the worst was still to come: "Mubarak went so far in disgrace to say that 'Israel had the right' to respond to Iraq [in case of a military attack] and that this would not change his position."[44] *Filasṭīn al-Muslima* still hoped that Mubarak would change his position before the journal reached the readers, but the magazine had to express its anger about the unlawful and stupid politics (*as-siyāsāt al-kharqā*)[45] that drove the *Umma* into such a state of discord.

The deception about the behaviour of the Muslims in the Gulf states was limitless. The "general, abundant joy" about the US-intervention among the Kuwaitis especially and the people of the Gulf states in general was "engendering grief" (*aṭārat istiyā'*) among Muslims in throughout the world.[46] Still, there were some lonely voices refusing the intervention of Western armies. However, King Fahd had threatened with the death penalty anybody who, according to the Islamists, "protests against this criminal war that was launched against a Muslim country by criminal hands".[47] Furthermore, his treacherous government published a text in the *Washington Post* to thank US President Bush and the American people for the liberation of Kuwait which included a map of the region on which the name of "Israel" was written on the territory of Palestine.[48]

Ḥamās addressed itself directly to the "Kuwaiti brothers" in a letter reminding them of their "links of blood and faith" with the Iraqi people as well as with the Palestinian community living in their country.[49] The believers should have been united in order to not allow the "unbelievers to spread corruption" (*fasād*) among them. Only in Jordan did both people and government support Iraq. While the country was militarily weak, it gained its power from the "palpitation of the streets that boils from hatred for the US and Israel".[50]

Criticism of the collaborating Arab regimes was virulent in *Filasṭīn al-Muslima*. From the material used for this analysis there was no indication that the "ontological-theological framework of analysis allows for little mention of the participation of Arab and Muslim troops in the anti-Iraq coalition" as advanced by Legrain.[51] On the contrary, their behaviour in the Gulf-crisis concretely confirmed the Islamists' criticism of certain Arab regimes as treacherous and non-Islamic, and the Islamists dwelled upon this abundantly. The events made the people sensitive to the core messages of the Islamists; if the rulers are deviant and act against the interests of their own people, as was the case in Egypt, the people become the "definitive government" (*ḥukūma maḥsūma*).[52] This is a reference to the ideas developed by Sayyid Qutb, who introduced the right to overthrow unjust rulers into Sunni Islamic thought. This is the main legitimation of the fundamentalists' struggle and they seized the occasion to renew their call to topple the existing regimes.

In this context, *Ḥamās* presented the good Muslim as an eternal being that can only feel and think in a certain way common to all of them. Thus the true Muslim is characterised by a "latent enmity" (*al-i'dā' al-kāmin*) against the United States and the West "which came to the fore now" (*fajara 'alanan*) in the "Arab and Muslim mentality" (*al nafsīya al-muslima al-arabīya*).[53] According to the Islamists' essentialist world view, individuals and nations are ascribed permanent and immutable qualities. Thus, Jews living today are always characterised by the features ascribed in the Qur'ān and the *Ḥadīth* to the Jewish opponents of the Prophet Muhammad in Medina. One of these features is the eternal struggle against Islam. In contrast to this, the characterisation of the Muslims as "latent enemies" of the Jews and the West has no basis whatsoever in the traditional Islamic texts. It can only be explained as a contemporary inversion of the well-known animosity of the Jews against the Muslims which was handed down through generations.

According to its strategy of playing the popular card opposed to the rulers, *Ḥamās* addressed itself directly to the Muslim peoples who were invited to exert pressure on their respective governments to end the participation of their armed forces in the Western-Arab-Alliance and to support the Iraqi people.[54] Furthermore, they were called to damage the interests of the "arrogance" (*istikbār*) everywhere in the world.[55] This term is often used to describe the Western powers that dominate and rule the world without respect for the interests of the Third World or countries of the southern hemisphere. "Arrogance" also has the religious connotation that it is one of the main features of the Jew's unchanging character according to ancient Islamic scriptures.[56] The Jews are said to have behaved arrogantly even with God Himself and to have rejected Him by distorting His message. Their refusal to accept the reign of Islam is further proof of the Jews' arrogance. So is the creation of the state of Israel. Thus the choice of the term *"istikbār"* is another expression of the overlapping of the two concepts of analysis: features of the traditional Islamic *Weltanschauung* are underlying the political analysis of international politics from a Third-World point of view.

The hostile reaction of the people – who are referred to by the term "the street" – against all that is Western and American is said to have surprised and frightened the West. The people made the West understand that its agents in the Middle East were in great danger.[57] Therefore the Western governments tried to get in touch with popular opposition forces. But unfortunately the US, who want to make Israel the super-state in the region, ignored the "total refusal of the state of Israel" by the ordinary Muslim.[58] Thus the United States – as well as their submissive regimes in the region – would be the loser of the ongoing war, no matter how it ends: "The true loss is the loss of the people, not the loss of a political regime".[59]

From *Ḥamās*' point of view, the Iraqi position on the Israeli-Palestinian conflict was crucial for opinion-making. The Iraqi missiles hitting Israel were said to have "positive effects" (*in'ikāsāt ījābīya*).[60] "For the first time since the creation of the "Zionist entitiy", its capital and other towns were hit so strongly. Thus the "Zionist deterrence strategy", based on the strenghth of the Israeli security service, was destroyed. The "illusion" (*wahm*) of the Six-Days-War was wiped out. Thus "the time of silence and fear" in dealing with Israel was over (...) and "the time of vengeance and the return to God began".[61] The Iraqi missiles launched on Israel are said to have shown a more effective way to win back Palestine than the proposed international conference.[62]

According to *Ḥamās*' vision that the struggle against the Jewish state is representative of the struggle of the *Umma* against Western domination, the missiles that hit Israel had an impact on the Muslims as a whole: the destruction of Israeli houses ended the Arab "resignation" (*al-ya's al-'arabī*).[63] "The first victim of the first Iraqi bomb hitting Tel Aviv was the Arab resignation, only in a second place did it kill Zionist people (...)".[64]The Iraqi bombing of Israeli territory destroyed the myth that the Israelis are militarily invulnerable. The "Iraqi Resistance"[65] showed that the *Umma*, if it possesses a common will, is capable of imposing its will on the world. As a result of this experience of their power, the Muslim people will no longer accept the "slavery chain" (*qayd al-'ubūdīya*)[66] of the West; they will destroy it and build their own "promising Islamic cultural project".[67]

Ḥamās thus celebrates the Iraqi attacks on Israel as a *revanche* for the humiliating Arab defeat against Israel in the Six-Days-War in 1967. By expressing these widespread popular feelings in spite of the fact that the Iraqi missiles never represented a serious threat for Israel, the Islamists further prove their psychological sensitivity and developed sense of honour. The defeat of Nasser against Israel was simultaneously recognised widely as the defeat of Arab secular nationalism which was perceived by the Islamists as being incapable of defending the Muslim interests in Palestine as the other "non-Islamic" ideologies and rulers in the Arab world. Still, the celebration of Saddam Hussein's policy as a "return of God" was surprising. Iraqi Ba'thism had always been an expression of secular Pan-Arabism, certainly not an ideology close to the Islamists' hearts. The idea that anybody believed in the seriousness of Saddam Hussein's newly discovered interest in Islam can certainly be excluded. Perhaps one possible explanation for the elevation of Saddam as a Muslim hero is the centrality of the Palestine question in Palestinian Islamism. Whoever seems to defend the Palestinian interests, a core duty for every true Muslim since it goes far beyond a simple territorial dispute, is accepted with open arms. The need to retain a grip on mass Palestinian opinion is a further explanation for the ideological inconsistency of embracing a longstanding enemy.

The Gulf War can be considered an unexpected "gift" for *Ḥamās* and other Islamist movememts in the Arab world, if this does not sound too dismissive of the many victims of this bloody confrontation. The events, with which most of the Arab Muslim people felt concerned, gave a boost to their movement since they clearly confirmed many of their positions. Thus the theme of the imperialist, colonial West fighting an eternal battle against the Islamic *Umma* dominated the conflict. The United States and the other Western states of the Alliance were again trying to impose their interests on the region. As the Arab Muslim world is extremely sensitive to the theme of Western domination and to any gesture that might be understood in this way, even people opposed to the Islamists in different times, like the Arab feminist quoted above, rally with them against Western military intervention. This explains the massive popular revolt which in no way means that all these people share the Islamists' views. But the latter made themselves the leaders of this widespread discontent in a skillfull manner.

Furthermore, the crisis confirmed the Islamists' preaching about the corrupt Arab regimes deviating from the true faith and selling the interests of the *Umma* for financial or other advantages. This was the evident case of Mubarak in Egypt and Asad in Syria, who joined the Alliance against their Iraqi brothers. This was also particularly true for the Saudi-Arabian and the Kuwaiti ruling families who invited the American troops to defend their thrones.[68]

Finally, the conflict gave the Islamists occasion to mobilise the masses for whom they always claimed to speak. The distinction between the rulers and the people in the Arab world, until then Islamist theory, became indeniable apparent in this conflict. As the Islamists rarely spend time dealing with nuances, they presented the whole Syrian people as siding with Iraq, the lack of manifestation of this solidarity being explained by the dictatorial regime making any popular demonstration impossible. The fundamentalist movements were often the only organised opposition in the Arab states, and so they almost automatically became the leaders of the popular contestation where it was expressed openly.

This explains the almost euphoric mood of *Ḥamās* when it spoke about the dawn of a new era. Finally, the public seemed to have got the Islamists' message about the need to take their fate into their own hands. The people decided to stand up and to overcome the resignation that has been characterising them for a long time. The importance accorded to the few Iraqi missiles that hit Israel can be compared to the psychological impact of the initial Arab dominance in the Arab-Israeli-War of 1973. The poor Iraqi soldiers were made heroes, the vanguard of the Arab nation. Their "success" confirmed the decision of the Palestinians in the Occupied Territories to fight the Israeli occupation physically. It was taken as a validation of the *Intifāḍa* and a reinforcement of *Ḥamās*' refusal of any negotiated solution. Little is said about the military defeat of Iraq nor about the fact that Israel could have responded in a severe manner to the Iraqi attacks. Facts were simply ignored. This is another example of the selective perception of reality by *Ḥamās*, a feature which should not be viewed as an incapacity, but as a method used deliberately in order to present handy slogans and theories.

NOTES

1. Iraq has accused Kuwait of having stolen oil from the Rumayla oil fields shortly after the end of the Iran-Iraq War, as well as keeping oil prices low through over-production. Only a week before, the Iraqi President Saddam Hussein had reassured the United States about his peaceful intentions.
2. Jordan, Sudan, Yemen and Mauritania abstained as well while Libya withdrew its delegation. Iraq was ineligible to vote. Thus 14 of the 21 members of the Arab league condemned the Iraqi invasion of Kuwait.
3. All together 28 countries participated in the alliance which was headed by the United States, Great Britain and France. On the Arab side Syria, Egypt, Saudi-Arabia and Kuwait participated in the military action against Iraq.
4. The articles in the book *Islamic Fundamentalisms and the Gulf Crisis*, edited by James Piscatori (1991), stress the pragmatic attitude of the Islamists during the Gulf War. Piscatori comes to the conclusion that the fundamentalists made compromises with the popular Muslim sentiment concerning Saddam Hussein and their Muslim patrons on whom they depend financially – thus proving their political flexibility.
5. The Kuwaitis claim to have given 60 million Dollars to *Ḥamās* and 27 million Dollars to the PLO in 1989. See Legrain, "A Defining Moment: Palestinain Islamic Fundamentalism", p. 79 in: Piscatori, *Islamic Fundamentalisms and the Gulf Crisis*, pp. 131–153.
6. See Philip Mattar, "The PLO and the Gulf Crisis," in: *Middle East Journal*, 48, no.1, Winter 1994, pp. 31–45 for the calculations and miscalculations of the PLO leadership in the Gulf crisis and the perception of its attitude in the West.
7. Legrain, "A Defining Moment. Palestinain Islamic Fundamentalism", in: Piscatori, *Islamic Fundamentalisms and the Gulf Crisis.* Legrain notes himself that in the magazine *Filasṭīn al-Muslima* the word "aggression" (*ghazw*) was used while the Jordanian Muslim Brotherhood made reference to the "entry" (*dukhūl*) of the Iraqi forces in their leaflet reproduced by *Ḥamās*. Ibid, p. 77, footnote 19.
8. Only in the leaflet no. 62 from 13 August 1990 does *Ḥamās* take official position in the Gulf conflict. The communiqué no. 61, even though dated from 3 August 1990 – one day after the Iraqi invasion – does not mention the events. The PLO – equally torn between diametrically opposed interests – only announced its official position on 19 August and in Arafat's speech on 29 August 1990. See Matar, *PLO and Gulf Crisis*, p. 34.
9. Leaflet *Ḥamās* no. 62, 13 August 1990. In: FM September 1990, p. 18. And the leaflet from 22 January 1991. In: FM February 1991, p. 65.
10. FM, February 1991, p. 7.
11. FM, February 1991, p. 14.

12. FM, February 1991, p. 7
13. *Bayān Ḥamās* no. 65, in FM, February 1991, p. 65.
14. FM, February 1991, p. 7.
15. Ibid.
16. FM, March 1991, p. 22.
17. FM, February 1991, p. 8.
18. FM, February 1991, p. 7.
19. FM, February 1991, p. 7.
20. FM, March 1991, p. 22ff. The following exposition is based on this article.
21. Ronald L. Nettler, "Arab Images of Jews and Israel", p. 35. In: *Survey of Jewish Affairs* (Oxford 1989), pp. 33–43.
22. FM, March 1991, p. 11.
23. *Bayān Ḥamās* no. 70. In: FM, March 1991, p. 6.
24. *Bayān Ḥamās* no. 62, 13.8.1990.
25. FM, February 1991, p. 7.
26. FM, March 1991, p. 23.
27. *Bayān Ḥamās* no. 62, 13.8.1990.
28. FM, March 1990, p. 36.
29. FM, March 1991, p. 1.
30. *Bayān* no. 70. In: FM, March 1991, p. 6.
31. *Bayān Ḥamās*, 22.1.1991. In: FM, February 1991, p. 65.
32. *Bayān Ḥamās*, 22.1.1991. In: FM, February 1991, p. 65.
33. *Bayān Ḥamās* no. 62, 13.8.1990.
34. The intrinsically expansionist nature of Zionism has at times been a common argument in secular Arab nationalism.
35. FM, March 1991, p. 36.
36. FM, March 1991, p. 1.
37. FM, March 1991, p. 1.
38. FM reproduces a leaflet issued by the Syrian Student Union calling the people to side with Iraq, February 1991, p. 15.
39. Ibid.
40. Ibid.
41. FM, February 1991, p. 7 and 15.
42. FM, February 1991, p. 7.
43. FM, February 1991, p. 15.
44. Ibid.
45. FM, February 1991, p. 7.
46. FM, February 1994, p. 14.
47. FM, February 1991, p. 14.
48. FM, July 1991, p. 65.
49. FM, May 1991, p. 7.
50. FM, February 1991, p. 15.
51. Legrain, "A Defining Moment: Palestinian Islamic Fundamentalism", p. 76.
52. FM, February 1991, p. 15.
53. FM, March 1991, p. 1.
54. *Bayān Ḥamās*, 22.1.1991. In: FM, February 1991, p. 65.
55. Ibid.

56. See Harkabi, op. cit., pp. 267/268.
57. FM, March 1991, p. 1.
58. Ibid.
59. FM, March 1991, p. 1.
60. FM, march 1991, p. 36.
61. FM, March 1991, p. 36/37.
62. FM, March 1991, p. 36.
63. FM, March 1991, p. 36.
64. Ibid.
65. FM, March 1991, p. 17.
66. FM, March 1991, p. 1.
67. Ibid. To validate this assertion the Qur'an (28,5) is quoted: "But it was our will to favour those who were oppressed and to make them leaders among men, to bestow on them a noble heritage and to give them power in the land." This verse, which is frequently quoted by the Islamists, is a useful tool in tranforming every defeat into an affirmation of the final victory of the Muslims.
68. Saudi-Arabia and the Gulf states were not considered very highly in the Arab-Muslim world even before the crisis; they were seen as lacking solidarity with their brothers in faith of the poorer Arab countries by not sharing their oil-based wealth with them.

CHAPTER TWELVE

Ḥamās and the Peace Process

THE AFTERMATH OF THE GULF WAR

After the defeat of Iraq in the Second Gulf War, the central question became the "new world order" as proposed by the American President George Bush. Within this framework, the Palestine question had a preeminent position. The Islamists emphasised that everybody first rejected the link which Saddam Hussein established between the Iraqi-Kuwaiti struggle and the Palestine question; then everybody accepted in one form or the other that the end of the "Palestine problem" was the only way to guarantee peace in the Middle East.[1]

Ḥamās judged this developmet as a "victory of Saddam"[2] and welcomed it because it conformed with their insistence on the centrality of the Palestine question for the Muslim world and thus the balance of power in the world. However, several factors meant that *Ḥamās'* analysis of the international environment and the critic of the inner-Palestinian decision making did not allow the hope that a negotiated solution would respect Islamic interests. Thus they firmly rejected any international conference or negotiated solution to the Palestine problem.

For *Ḥamās*, there was no doubt that the new international security order was a purely "American system" with the main goal to cement the hegemonious position of the Zionist entity in the region.[3] Any negotiations under the auspices of the United States were necessarily rejected,a position derived from the Qur'anic verse "Put no trust in the wrongdoers, lest the Fire should touch you. None but God can protect or help you."[4] The other aim was the suppression of the Islamic awakening (*ṣaḥwa*).[5] The Islamists reproached the US for inventing scenarios for the Middle East "as if they were God,"[6] and treating the people in the region as a "bunch of sheep"[7] and "playing in almost total freedom with the fate of the *Umma*".[8]

Ḥamās was afraid that the region was standing in front of an "enlarged Camp David".[9] The separate peace treaty between Egypt and Israel from 1978 was considered a betrayal of Muslim interests by so-called Muslim leaders and a shameful defeat in the struggle with the enemy. It was concerned that the Arab states that were asking for an international conference under the auspices of the United Nations did not recognise the decisive changes in the international system since the collapse of the Soviet Union.[10] The Soviet Union being no longer a superpower, any international conference would take place in the "shadow of the US".[11] The United Nations, who had in former times been a forum representing Third World interests, was only defending US-interests in the Islamists' eyes. The abandoning of the besieged Bosnian Muslims and the UN's demand that Iraq's chemical and nuclear programme was dismantled while Israel could develop those weapons without any control, confirmed the Islamists' conviction that double standards were applied by the UN as a result of its domination by the US and other Western powers. This criticism of the United Nations was far from being a specific Islamist conviction; the debate about the future of this international institution shows the enormous discontent of almost the entire southern hemisphere with its functioning and with the historical privileges for certain northern, industrialised states. By refusing to acknowledge the legitimacy of the UN in its present form, *Ḥamās* again voiced a widespread, if not mainstream, disillusionment and its discourse overlapped with other Third-World discourses. For *Ḥamās*, there were enough historical examples to prove that any siding with the US and the big powers was no alternative to struggle and confrontation: The fate of Muhammad Ali in Egypt, Ataturk in Turkey, Reza Pahlevi in Iran and "a dozen others" showed clearly that this path always ends in more oppression from and dependence on the West.[12]

As more time went by and as the shuttle diplomacy of the US-foreign minister James Baker became more intensive, the more *Ḥamās* was validated in its rejection of the peace process: Israel opposed any participation of PLO members in the negotiation and would not suffer any pressure from the US to change her position. UN resolutions no 242 und 338 were still the subject of discussion and would not be applied.[13] The status of Jerusalem would not even be discussed. *Ḥamās* described the regional conferences and the settlement plan as a "war with other means"[14] undertaken by the US and Israel.

In a communiqué *Ḥamās* called the period the "darkest in Arab-Islamic history" because almost "no voice" was "standing up against the deluge that carries away the Arab and Islamic organisations" supporting the "liquidation" (*taṣfiya*) of the Palestine question.[15] It refused to join the "defeatist discourse" (*manṭiq al-taswiya*) about an agreement because it would involve the surrender of Arab and Palestinian rights which is excluded by the Sharī'a and the Islamic creed.[16] The organisation drew an historical line by declaring that all religious *Fatwas* since the 1920s excluded such a settlement; they were said to present *Jihād* as the only method to handle the problem because it avoids the recognition of the Jewish presence in Palestine. It asked the PLO to be in "harmony" (*insijām*) with the position of the Palestinian people by rejecting the "conference for selling the territory" (*mu'tamar li bay 'al-arḍ*) which is called the "peace conference" in order to cover the truth.[17] In its communiqué issued to celebrate the fifth anniversary of the *Intifāḍa*, *Ḥamās* asserted that the "people" would never accept an end to the *Intifāḍa* in submission to the US-will.[18]

The Supreme Leader of the Muslim Brothers in Egypt, Muhammad Hamid Abul Nasr expressed his "great fear" about the proposed peaceful solutions which were said to give advantages to the Jews.[19] He reiterated the refusal of the Muslim Brotherhood to recognise the "Zionist enemy" and to bargain over the territory of Palestine which were equal to the bargaining over the Islamic Sharī'a and creed. In the end, the Supreme Leader called for the support of *Ḥamās*.

Filasṭīn al-Muslima repeatedly denounced the Israeli intentions. The "Zionist enemy" did not really want peace; he was "without any interest in it".[20] At the same time, Israel was said to be interested in certain advantages such as the end of the state of war with its neighbours, better relations with them in order to profit from its markets and to decrease the importance of the Islamic groups opposing any agreement.[21] But Israel would consider peace to be merely a "temporary stage" in its strategy of economic and cultural expansion.[22] It needed a pause in order to successfully integrate the Jews that immigrated from the former Soviet Union.[23]

This further illustrates the two main characteristics which the Islamic fundamentalists attribute to the Jews: their striving for expansion and their falseness. Therefore *Ḥamās* preferred the "prolongation of the present situation with all its weaknesses" to joining the US-Zionist arrangement because they believed that the present weakness of the Muslims will be followed by a period of strength – "this is the logic of history".[24] Again, the Qur'ānic verse "But it was our will to favour those who where oppressed and to make them leaders among men" was quoted.[25] As a contemporary example of the anticipated decline of the once dominating powers, the fate of the Soviet Union was mentioned. Its sudden disappearance was to be a "lesson" for those who believe in the power of the US and in the continuity of its hegemony.[26]

Underlying the use of this Qur'ānic verse is the Islamic experience and theory of history. The Prophet Muhammad and his followers were being oppressed in Mekka and so fled to Medina only to come back a few years later as victor, God having bestowed his favour on those true believers. History being perceived as the expression and confirmation of faith, Muslims will be extremely sucessful on earth the day they return to their religion. Faith being expressed more in deeds than in belief in Islam, true Muslims have to strive for the establishment of an ideal society on earth according to God's will and therefore must be succesful in contemporary international politics. At the same time, this is another example of *Ḥamās'* ability to mix Islamic ideas with a political analysis of the contemporary situation. The sudden and unexpected breakdown of the Soviet Union was mentioned as a confirmation of the Islamic truth that in the long run the Islamic creed would triumph over all other systems of thought and religion. This skillful interweaving of two different systems of thought made their discourse appeal to an enlargened strata of population and again shows *Ḥamās'* modern character. *Ḥamās'* reaction to the development was the opening of a "new phase" of the *Intifāḍa*, called the "war of the knives."[27] In the meantime, however, the development took a different turn on the international level.

THE BEGINNING OF THE PEACE CONFERENCE IN MADRID, 30 OCTOBER 1991

On 30 October 1991, the Middle East Peace Conference opened in the Royal Palace in Madrid. The Palestinians participated in a joint Jordanian-Palestinian delegation without any members of the PLO – thus fulfilling the Israeli conditions. Israel, Egypt, Syria and Lebanon were present, each with their own delegations. The conference was convened by Gorbatschow and US-President Bush, and not under the auspices of the United Nations as demanded by the Arab side. The PNC approved the Palestinian participation in the peace process at its meeting in Algiers on 23 September. On 17 October, the PLO Central Committee gave its consent to the participation of the Palestinians in a joint delegation with Jordan.

Most alarmed, *Ḥamās* issued its "Declaration for History" in the forefront of the planned conference, virulently denouncing the peace process.[28] The region was said to be in a dangerous situation unequalled in history: the Islamic *Umma* never ever surrendered to the enemy.[29] The goal of the conference, held by the United States, was sait to be to "liquidate the Palestine question" and to create the "Thora inspired dream" (*ḥulmuhu al-tūrātī*) of what is called "Greater Israel" from the Nile to the Euphrates.[30] The conference aimed to grant international legality to the "Zionist entity" and end the Arab boycott so that it could play a dangerous role in the Arab region.[31] All this was "clear as the sun at four o'clock in the afternoon".[32] The most that "the enemies of God and humanity" could propose, was a sort of "self-government" (*ḥukm dhātī*) for the Palestinian inhabitants who do not possess the territory (*sukkān dūn al-arḍ*).[33] Thus "we are asked to sign our death sentence ourselves".[34] The Madrid opening session was said to be a "festivity to make Arabs believe that their dreams of liberation were still within reach and that the Arab delegations in Madrid will realise what forty years of armed struggle failed to do".[35]

The opposition to the conference and the criticism of the PNC and the PLO for approving the peace process were based on different levels of analysis: the theological and the political. Referring to Islamic theological teaching, the peace process was interpreted as the continuation of the Western "conspiracy" or "plot" (*tamurru al mu'āmara*);[36] only this time "certain Arab organisations and leaderships (PLO) bless the gradual capitulation" (*tubāriku al khaṭawāt al istislāmiya*) of the Palestinians. The "frantic competition" of certain Palestinians and Arabs to "comply to the US-Zionist idolatry" (*shirk*) was denounced. The *Umma* was called to say its word and "not to lead certain leaders to falsify its will". It was reminded of its religious duty to participate in the decisive struggle with the "enemy of God and humanity". Any concession was considered as "vain" (*bāṭil*) and not binding to any Muslim.[37] The acceptance of the conference and negotiations was even called "treason against God and His Messenger"[38] and treason against the "thousands of martyrs and wounded and arrested that defended the honor of their people" (*karāma*).[39]

This commentary clearly places these political developments in the fundamentalist world view. The peace conference was seen merely as a new chapter in the eternal battle between good and evil, between righteousness and falsehood, between Islam and the other religions, sects and ideologies, between *ḥaqq* and *bāṭil*. The terms "plot" and "conspiracy" clearly marked the historical continuity with the Jewish opposition against the Prophet Muhammad in early Islam. Since then these same enemies were – under different disguises such as imperialism, communism, nationalism – trying to harm the Muslims in a "hydra-type conspiracy"[40].

The Christians and Jews were thus seen as united in their ingratitude to God. The use of the term *shirk* in connection with the US and Zionism is nevertheless initially astonishing. *Shirk* is often mentioned in the later Suras of the Qur'ān where it means polytheism and idolatry. The worshipping of another besides God directly defies the centre piece of the Islamic message, the oneness of God. Thus Muhammad declared it a sin for which God has no forgiveness.[41] In mainstream theology, Christians and Jews as "people of the book" – who believe in one God even though they distorted his message – have not been considered as *mushrikūn*. This term was only applied to pagans and adherents of all other beliefs and certainly never to other Muslims.[42] The fundamentalists definitely did not go back to this original use of the term *shirk*, despite their claim to dig up the original concepts and meanings of Islam.

In the course of the dogmatic development of Islam and the establishment of different Muslim sects, the meaning of the term *shirk* has been considerably expanded and has even become a reproach made by one Muslim against another.[43] Sayyid Qutb gave the concept a more radical stance for contemporary use in connection with his reinterpretation of *Jāhiliyya*: the mere recognition of God's existence does not exclude polytheist violation if His absolute authority is not respected in all affairs, including worldly ones. For Qutb, the new idols were materialism and egoism, but also ideologies like nationalism or democracy with institutions like parliaments and supreme courts or elsewhere dictators being turned into ultimate sources of authority instead of God. (It is important to remember that the Palestinian Islamists – contrasting with other fundamentalist Islamic groups in the Arab world – do not include democracy in these vices.) Even in Islamic societies, this development has taken place so that they have reverted in Qutb's eyes to "polytheism" and therefore to *Jāhiliyya*, the pre-Islamic period of ignorance of the godly revelation. Thus in contemporary Islamic radicalist thought, polytheism (*shirk*) has become the simple expression of all non-Islamist approach to politics, ethics and economics. This is the way it was used by *Ḥamās* when it accused the US, Zionists and certain Arab leaders in one breath of idolatry. The use of this Islamic term had obvious advantages: the very general and imprecise meaning in its new interpretation allowed the Islamists to remain vague in their reasoning while touching most Muslim-educated people on an emotional level. Despite the evolution of its meaning, for many Muslims *shirk* is synonymous with the worst sin of a human being, the non-recognition of the oneness of God, and can easily be presented as a threat to everyone who believes that he is a Muslim.

In the Islamists' dualistic world view there cannot be compromise between the two antagonistic forces involved in the fight for world domination. It is a struggle for survival which can only admit one victor. Voluntary capitulation on the part of the Muslims cannot be permitted as they are foreseen as victors in the sacred master plan for history; if they return to their religion and express their faith through truly Muslim behaviour and politics. Thus the acceptance of talks about a compromise was just another proof for the deviation and corruption of the concerned political Arab leaders who did not behave nor rule according to Islamic law. On the contrary, they were committing "treason" against God in the same way that Jews and Christians were doing it. The pursuance of these ungodly aims is *bāṭil* (vain, unreal) as opposed to *ḥaqq*.

Translated into juridical terms, *bāṭil* means that any concession or agreement based on concession is null and void, withhout legal effect and therefore not binding for Muslims. In the Hanafi school, a legal act judged *bāṭil* means to be of the most extreme nullity. It is considered as non-existent if one of the elements essential for the existence of any legal activity is lacking, such as the free will of the two parties – in contrast to a *fāsid* act that exists, although it is vitiated and therefore needs to be negated. *Ḥamās* thus transformed its conviction that the integrity of a Muslim Palestine is part of the Islamic creed in Muslim law. The Islamists' belief that God wants the Muslims to rule on earth became legal status as opposed to international law. In fact, the decision to make peace with Israel was considered merely a "political opinion", but the "violation of historical, religious and national rights" could not be considered a simple matter of freedom of political thought.[44]

Therefore Muslims are obliged to fight the concession of any inch of Palestinian soil. As I have already discussed, the *Jihād* on behalf of Palestine is a religious duty for all Muslims according to most modernist and fundamentalist interpretations of *Jihād*. When the *Umma* was called to "say its word" to prevent any leader falsifying its will, the Islamists certainly had in mind the powerful street demonstrations in various Arab countries during the Gulf crisis that obliged governments, and the fundamentalist opposition itself, to change their initial political line for a more pro-Iraqi attitude. *De facto*, only *Ḥamās* remained in opposition to the series of concessions to Israel. The "brothers of Ibn Taymiyya and Izz ad-Din al-Qassam" were called to guide the people in their *Jihād* against this "injustice" (*ẓulm*) and in their struggle to restore "the real" (*ḥaqq*).[45] *Ḥaqq* meaning the real, permanent, fixed reality as designed by God. *Al-ḥaqq* is often used as a name of God in the sense that he is the absolute real while other beings depend for their reality on him. *Ḥaqq* signifies the establishment of a society and community on earth according to divine law and guidance. It means the redressing of history to make it concordant with the Divine Providence.

Parallel to this theological argumentation, *Ḥamās* expressed its criticism of the Palestinian National Congress, which accepted the peace negotiations, in very different terms. It demanded a more democratic decision-making and thus again reveals itself to be a modern political opposition force. The PNC in its present form was rejected because it still worked according to a quota system, members being appointed, and it did not include any person from within the Occupied Territories. It had "no right to take decisions in the name of the Palestinians"[46] because in its present form it did not at all represent the forces leading the "daily and bloody Resistance" against occupation. "The absence of numerous Palestinian forces active in the national Palestinian fight from the decision making" was mentioned again in a later communiqué[47] as the first reason for the non-binding character of any PNC-decision. Therefore the PNC's consent did not mean the agreement of the "entire Palestinian population".[48] The upright members of the PNC were asked to side with their people and to boycott the institution.[49]

The rejection of the PNC in its present form was no new element in the discourse of the Islamists. The Islamists did not question the institution itself, but rather the undemocratic and unrepresentative process of its formation.[50] The necessity to transform the PNC into a "real representation of all stratas of our people", those living inside the Territories and those in the diaspora, appeared to be one of the most urgent demands of *Ḥamās*.[51] It called for elections based on the principle of "proportional representation" (*al-tamthīl an-nisbī*).[52] The approval of the Palestinian participation in the peace conference "based on US-Zionist conditions" entirely discredited the PNC in the eyes of the Islamists. It "frustrated the hopes of the Palestinians" and "neglected their rights".[53]

This is completely in line with former positions of *Ḥamās*. Earlier it had declared that all those who agreed to meet the US foreign secretary James Baker on his visits to the region were said not to represent in any way the Palestinian people and its will.[54] *Fataḥ*, which was the only Palestinian organisation meeting Baker, was called in another place a "cancerous tumour" (*waram saraṭāni*) destroying the Palestinian body.[55] Thus the question "Who represents the Palestinians?" was clearly answered: it is the "Palestinian people",[56] "the common man" (*rajul basīṭ*), "the street" (*shāriʿ*)[57] and not the PNC nor *Fataḥ*.

The criticism of the non-democratic character of the Palestinian national institutions in exile could be seen as a clear expression of *Ḥamās'* will to participate in them. In this part of their discourse there is no trace of the Qutbian concept of *al-ḥākimiyya* that denounces all man-made decisions and institutions and is according the total sovereignty and rule to God alone. Their call for a "truly representative" parliament was far from being an isolated cry from those who were excluded. There was a chorus of voices demanding an urgent reshaping of the Palestinian national institutions, among them the voice of Jamil Hilal, then director of the PLO Information Department in Tunis and member of the PNC.[58] His analysis of the ossification of the PLO structures and its incapacity to adapt under the impact of the *Intifāḍa* contained exactly the same demands for wide-ranging reconstruction that *Ḥamās* put forward. He denounced the unrepresentative character of the PNC whose appointed members were merely providing legitimacy to political deals reached by the leadership of the various Resistance movements united in the PLO.[59] The personality cult, the autocratic decision-making, the patronage and corruption within this heavy bureaucracy were widely and strongly denounced as well as the non-representation of the Occupied Territories despite six years of *Intifāḍa* and three years of peace negotiations.[60]

Ḥamās thus voiced a widespread discontent in the Occupied Territories with the functioning of the Palestinian national institutions. This guaranteed the organisation much popular support. The clever link between this call for reforms and the insistence on the non-binding character of PNC decisions appealed to all those Palestinians who were less sensible to the religious reasons for the rejection of the peace conference.

At the same time, the Islamists mixed the widely shared criticism of the lack of democracy in the Palestinian national institutions with a populism that also has undemocratic features. The outcry that not "all Palestinians" agreed with the accords could not in itself be a reason to reject them because in a democracy the majority decides against the will of a minority. The entire population will never agree on something. The vision of unanimity that the Islamists seemed to propose is unrealistic and sheds new doubts on their understanding of democracy.

This is all the more true as *Ḥamās* then left the pseudo-democratic discourse behind in order to switch again without transition to another set of conviction and beliefs: it was "warning those who talk and bargain over our Palestine and *al-Aqṣā*"[61] that their doing so would have consequences. Those consequences were made clear by reminding them of the "fate of Sadat" (*maṣīr as-Sādāt*).[62] The warning went on to say that the "*Umma* is not sleeping and History has no mercy" and among our people there are "thousands of Islambulis".[63] Islambuli, a lieutenant in the Egyptian army and member of the Islamist organisation *al-Jihād al-Islāmi*, killed the Egyptian President Anwar el-Sadat in October 1981 because of his decision to recognise and make peace with Israel in 1978. Sadat was accused by the Islamists at that time of being an "infidel" or a "corrupt tyrant": if he believed that the Camp David accords were permissible, he was a *kāfir*; if he was convinced of the wrongness of the agreement, he was a *fāsiq ẓālim*[64].

Ḥamās' discourse was again based on a reinterpretion of traditional Islamic texts and doctrines. The idea that a Muslim ruler who in the eyes of his critics does not act according to Islamic regulation can legitimately be murdered cannot be found in Islamic theological tradition. It is a new creation based on the teachings of Sayyid Qutb and further developed by 'Abd As-Salam Faraj, the ideologue of *al-Jihād al-Islāmī*. In giving universal validity to the meaning of *jāhiliyya*, Qutb denounced the existing Muslim governments and societies as *jāhil*. Only through *Jihād* could the sovereinty of God (*ḥākimiyya*) be restored. This call for *Jihād* has been radicalised by Faraj in his booklet "The Neglected Duty" (*al-farīda al-ghā'iba*) by narowing its scope to military fight especially directed against infidel rulers who stand in the way of creating a divine state by their failure to apply God's law. Those rulers are as infidel as the Mongols were in the times of Ibn Taymiyya and it is the duty of Muslims to fight them without delay and without compromise. This definition of *Jihād* as the simple assasination of a Muslim ruler is a most contemporary and free reinterpretation of the Islamic concept of *Jihād*, reached through an extremely selective interpretation of original texts and misunderstanding of the terms.[65] It was applied by Islambuli with the murdering of Sadat and serves as an example to other radical Islamist groups.

Still, the main focus of the *Ḥamās' Jihād* is the Israeli enemy and its form the *Intifāḍa*. The ending of the popular uprising must be avoided by any means. An article entitled "Will the *Intifāḍa* be the first victim of the settlement?" appeared in *Filasṭīn al-Muslima*.[66] The *Intifāḍa*, glorified as the expression of the will of "the people" and led by the squadrons of "*al-Qassām*", was considered by *Ḥamās* as its exclusive political scene. It created the close link between the Islamic Resistance Movement and the people which the organisation constantly plays off against the PLO to ensure its legitimate right to speak for the Palestinians. Thus the armed Resistance in the Territories is vital for *Ḥamās* and its political future. Only the *Intifāḍa* allows them to stand up against the PLO and to fight its right to represent the Palestinians. In the future, power sharing in whatever Palestinian entity might be created is essential. Hence the insistence on the continuation of the armed struggle against Israel has to be seen first of all in the light of political concurrence of two parties struggling for the support of the people. For this reason, *Ḥamās'* insistence on *Jihād* must not remain an obstacle to any solution in the conflict. The oft-proven pragmatism of the Islamic Resistance Movement makes it probable that the armed struggle might be abandoned when their political influence is secured otherwise.[67] In their selective and arbitrary use of Islamic sources, the Islamists will certainly find a theological justification for such a manoeuvre.

Ḥamās invokes the international Islamic movement against the alleged international conspiracy. It should have played its "natural role" by rejecting this conference and by taking all possible ways and means to make it fail.[68] The "International Conference in Support of the Islamic Revolution in Palestine" organised in Teheran (19–24 October 1991) was a powerful demonstration of this *Islamic Internationale*. 800 delegates from 60 countries participated, among them *Ḥamās*, but also members of the main fractions of the constitutent PLO groups. On the last day of the conference, *Ḥamās*, together with nine other Palestinian organisations, signed a "historic document"[69] refusing the Palestinian participation in the "so-called" peace conference and calling for the continuation of the *Intifāḍa* and the "escalation" (*taṣa'ād*) of military actions against the enemy.[70]

This opposition to the peace conference led to an intensified cooperation with other Islamic groups such as the "Islamic Jihad". The Teheran conference and the numerous joint communiqués showed this clearly.[71] The sense of urgency among the Islamists confronted with what they considered a "sell-out" of Muslim rights must have been enormous. Until the peace conference, *Ḥamās* and the "Islamic Jihad" had hardly been cooperating because concurrence in the power struggle often bore more weight than the common political goal, the destruction of Israel.

Also, the preachers in the mosques of the entire Muslim world are called to "shed light on the conspiracy" and to make the believers understand its "dimensions and dangers".[72] Muslims were urged to understand that the Palestinian community not only risked the loss of their homeland forever; but that the fate of Palestine and the holy sites was linked to the struggle of the Muslim world community to win back the leading role in the world. Believing that public opinion could still influence the course of events – as was demonstrated during the Gulf crisis – *Ḥamās* renewed its attacks on the Arab mass media whose most powerful role in modern societies had always been acknowledged by the Islamists. It attacked the Arab media for "deforming the truth" and trying to "turn upside down the truth" in their efforts to create an Arab public opinion supportive of the negotiations.[73]

Ḥamās knew that the Palestinians in the Occupied Territories were longing for better living conditions and more respect in daily life. Thus any – even illusionary – promises of political leaders about an improvement on these two levels in case of a peace treaty would appeal to the population and make them willing to give a substantial change a chance. This would mean a concurrent decline of support for the oppositional discourse proposed by *Ḥamās*. Therefore it was essential for the organisation to spread its view of the harmful consequences of the peace conference. However, the subservience of the Arab media to the respective political rulers left no voice to political opposition such as the Islamists. Thus the public prayers in the mosques were an efficient tool for spreading the Islamists' message.[74]

NOTES

1. FM, April 1991, p. 8.
2. FM, April 1991, p. 8.
3. FM, April 1992, p. 1.

4. Qur'ān 11, 113 quoted in communiqué *Ḥamās* no. 71. In: FM, March 1991, p. 7.
5. FM, April 1991, p. 14.
6. FM, March 1991, p. 6.
7. FM, April 1991, p. 7.
8. FM, May 1991, p. 1.
9. FM, April 1991, p. 8.
10. FM, March 1991, p. 17.
11. Ibid.
12. FM, June 1991, p. 28.
13. FM, June 1991, p. 28.
14. FM, June 1991, p. 28.
15. FM, July 1991, p. 38.
16. Ibid.
17. *Bayān Ḥamās* no. 77. In: FM, September 1991, p. 5.
18. In: FM January 1992, p. 5.
19. Communiqué 26.5.1991. In: FM, July 1991, p. 37/37. This statement is quoted in a communiqué of *Ḥamās* underlining the close parental link between the Muslim Brotherhood in Egypt and *Ḥamās*. In: FM, July 1991, p. 38/39.
20. FM, January 1992, p. 8.
21. Ibid.
22. FM, December 1991, p. 9.
23. Ibid.
24. Unnumbered communiqué. In: FM, July 1991, p. 39.
25. Qur'ān 28,5. In: FM, October 1993, p. 3.
26. *Bayān Ḥamās* no. 79. In: FM, November 1991, p. 5.
27. The stabbing of Israelis within Israel, mainly Jerusalem, started after the bloody clashes of 8 October 1990 in Jerusalem which resulted in 21 Palestinian deaths and nearly 150 wounded.
28. Dated 23.9.1991. In: FM, October 1991, p. 65.
29. Ibid.
30. *Bayān Ḥamās* no. 78. In: FM, October 1991, p. 5.
31. Ibid.
32. "Declaration for History" of *Ḥamās*. In: FM, October 1991, p. 65.
33. *Bayān Ḥamās* no. 78. In: FM. October 1991, p. 5.
34. "Declaration for History" of *Ḥamās*. In: FM, October 1991, p. 65.
35. Editorial FM, December 1991, p. 1.
36. "Declaration for History" of *Ḥamās*, 23.9.1991. In: FM, October 1991, p. 65. The following quotations are taken from this text.
37. *Bayān Ḥamās* no. 80. In: FM, December 1991, p. 5.
38. *Bayān Ḥamās* no. 78. In: FM, October 1991, p. 5.
39. *Bayān Ḥamās* no. 79. In: FM, November 1991, p. 5.
40. Choueiri, *Islamic Fundamentalism*, p. 94.
41. Sura 6, 51 and 116; Sura 31, 13; Sura 21, 22.
42. However, some commentators interpreted Sura xcviii, in the sense that the term *mushrikūn* includes "the people of the book". Generally the term

kāfir has been used for unbelievers including the *mushrikūn* and "the people of the book". See *Encyclopaedia of Islam*.

43. See its use by Mu'tazilis and Almohares.
44. Undated joint communiqué *Ḥamās*, DFLP and PFLP. In: FM, November 1991, p. 17.
45. "Declaration for History" of *Ḥamās*. In: FM, October 1991, p. 65. The Hanbalite jurist Ibn Taymiyya is a common reference in Islamist thought and writing as he denounced the Mongols of the 14th century – despite their conversion to Islam – of living in a state of apostasy because they continued to apply their customary law. Therefore it was a religious obligation for true Muslims to fight the Mongol until they abide to the Sharia. Today's Islamists dwell on these teachings in their fight against nominally Muslim regimes. 'Izz ad-Din al-Qassam is a more local reference of Palestinian Islamists: he had been the first leader of armed resistence against the British and the Jews in Palestine.
46. "Declaration for History" of *Ḥamās*. In: FM, October 1991, p. 65.
47. Joint communique *Ḥamās*, *al-Jihād al-Islāmi*, and other non-Islamic organisations opposing the peace process, 9 October 1991. In: FM, November 1991, p. 23.
48. FM, October 1991, p. 15.
49. "Declaration for History" of *Ḥamās*. In: FM, October 1991, p. 65.
50. In a meeting between PLO-chairman Arafat and the spokesman of *Ḥamās*, Ibrahim Ghusha, in Khartoum on 7 September 1991, the Islamic organisation repeated its condition for participation in the PNC: free elections, otherwise *Ḥamās* should get at least 40 percent of the seats.(Earlier *Ḥamās* had been asking for 50 percent of the seats.) Any common political programme has to include the rejection of the UN-resolutions no. 242, 181, 338 and the refusal to recognise Israel. In order to realise efficiently the resistence, *Ḥamās* would be ready to enter the PNC under these conditions. See "Declaration for History" of *Ḥamās*. In: FM, October 1991, p. 65.
51. Undated joint communiquè of *Ḥamās*, *al-Jihād al-Islāmi* and other non-Islamic organisations opposing the peace process. In: FM, November 1991, p. 17.
52. Ibid.
53. *Bayān Ḥamās* no. 79. In: FM, November 1991, p. 5.
54. *Bayān Ḥamās* no. 77. In: FM, September 1991, p. 5.
55. FM, May 1991, p. 13.
56. Ibid.
57. FM, April 1991, p. 22.
58. Jamil Hilal, "PLO Institutions: The Challenge Ahead", in: *Journal of Palestine Studies*, Autumn 1993, no. 1, pp. 46–60.
59. Ibid, p. 58.
60. Ibid, p. 59.
61. *Bayān Ḥamās* no. 80. In. FM, December 1991, p. 5.
62. Ibid.
63. Ibid.

64. Following a statement of Sheikh Salah Abu Isma'il, a supporter of *al-Jihād al-Islāmi*, in the trial of the organisation.
65. See on Faraj's selective method and his use of Ibn Taymiyya: Nazih N. Ayubi, *Political Islam. Religion and Politics in the Arab World*, London/New York 1991, p. 144.
66. November 1991, p. 26.
67. See Sheikh Yassin's proposal of a "truce" with Israel in exchange for its withdrawl from the Occupied Territories.
68. *Bayān Ḥamās* no. 80. In: FM, December 1991, p. 5.
69. The Teheran-document is characterised like this in the *Bayān Ḥamās* no. 80. In: FM, December 1991, p. 5.
70. Joint communiqué of the 10 Palestinian groups. In: FM, November 1991, p. 31.
71. Abu-Amr talks about "considerable progress (...) in improving the relations with the 'Islamic Jihad'". "Hamas: A historical and political background", p. 19. In: *Journal of Palestine Studies*, Autumn 1991, no. 4, p. 5–19.
72. Ibid.
73. FM, December 1991, p. 2.
74. See Beverly Milton-Edwards description of the practical programme of opposition accompanying the process of dialogue. In newspapers, audio-cassette, leaflets etc *Ḥamās* discerned the humiliation of Islam in every aspect of the talks, from the date of the first meeting to the choice of hotels. "Political Islam in Palestine in an environment of peace?", p. 202, in: *Third World Quarterly*, Volume 17, No. 2,(1996), pp. 199–225.

Chapter Thirteen

The Mass Deportation of Islamists to South-Lebanon in December 1992

Following the murder of a kidnapped Israeli paramilitary boarder guard, Israel expelled 415 Palestinians to South Lebanon in December 1992. Most of them were allegedly associated with Islamist movements, mainly with *Ḥamās*, who had claimed responsibility for the killing of the boarder guard. None of the Palestinians had been tried or formally charged with an offence. The UN Security Council unanimously condemned the deportation in resolution no 799 and demanded the "immediate and safe return" of all deportees. Israel's violation of the Fourth Geneva Convention from 12 August 1949 was stated. The PLO left the peace talks in Washington in protest, the ongoing eighth round was interrupted. By vigorously defending the Islamists and its internal opponents, the PLO tried to emphasise its claim to represent the entire Palestinian population. But *Ḥamās* took the greatest advantage from the arbitrary Israeli decision: the discipline and fortitude of the deportees, refusing to accept any compromise solution, surviving and praying in snow-storms without medical aid and with little food, increased the standing and legitimacy of the *Ḥamās*-movement in Palestinian, Arab and even world opinion. The United States and Israel announced on 1 February a deal which allowed the return of one hundred deportees and reduced the length of the banishment of the remaining Palestinians to a maximum of 12 months. This was presented by the US as the beginning of the implementation of UN-resolution no. 799 and therefore the resumption of the peace talks was urged. The Security Council accepted this interpretation on 12 February and the Palestinian negotiating camp was put in a difficult position: Palestinian public opinion rejected the resumption of the peace talks that had not brought any progress since their beginning a year ago. On the 27 April the Palestinian side finally returned to the negotiating table in Washington while the majority of the deportees still remained in South Lebanon.

The arbitrary mass deportation and the enclosing of the Occupied Territories was interpreted by *Ḥamās* as a "proof of the depth of the hysteria" of the Zionist enemy.[1] It again showed that the war with him was a "war for survival and existence" (*ḥarb baqā' wa-wujūd*).[2] In a *Ḥamās* memorandum addressed to the Palestinian leadership in Tunis, the mass deportation was interpreted as reaffirming the "views that the Zionists have towards our people", the "non-respect of any international laws and accords by the enemy" and therefore the "impossibility of making peace with them".[3] It was seen as "pàrt of the Zionists' resettlement policy that has no limits". *Ḥamās* called for the "immediate and definitive retreat"[4] from the negotiations and the escalation of the *Intifāḍa*.

The events seemed to confirm *Ḥamās'* characterisation of Israel and the Jews. Hysterical in their eternal enmity towards and contempt for the Muslims, the Jews were vicious and treacherous – as laid down in the Qur'ān and the *Hadīth*. While supposedly negotiating a peace agreement, they created facts on the ground by deporting several hundreds of Palestinians from their homeland. What better proof of their disinterest in a genuine reconciliation could the Jews bring? Violating the Geneva Convention on how to deal with the population of militarily occupied territories as well as UN-resolution no. 242 and then no. 799, the Israelis could not be trusted. The supposedly religious justifications advanced by certain nationalist religious Jews such as Rabbi Shlomo Aviner for not respecting international law confirmed the Islamists' view.[5] Vicious by nature and trying to harm mankind, the Jews would also violate any settlement of the Palestine question that might be found. The Israelis' behaviour therefore proved *Ḥamās'* claim that the Muslims should not negotiate with Israel, but should fight it; a military defeat being the only means to make them abandon their attempts to harm the Muslims.

Since deportations are an extremely sensitive point for Palestinians, who have been traumatised by mass deportations since 1948, the greatest expulsion in numbers of Palestinians since 1967 could easily be presented as a vital threat for Palestinian "survival and existence". As the "Zionist entity" was seeking expansion, according to the Islamists' view, the mass expulsion was presented as a first step in this design. Here the Islamists were voicing the mainstream feeling of the Palestinian population in those days.[6] The deportation was perceived by the population as a "signal that their 'transfer' from their homeland had now begun".[7] It thus reminded the Palestinians of the fate that could be waiting for them if they did not defend themselves against the Israeli aggression - thus illustrating the vision painted by *Ḥamās*.

At the same time, the Israeli overreaction confirmed the Islamists' conviction that the actions of the *Mujāhidūn* hit the "fundament of the false entity" and that they were the only effective means to fight the occupation.[8] Furthermore, only miltary blows against Israel and the reaction they trigger off showed the true face of Israel to the Muslims who might otherwise have been willing to believe in the Israelis' interest in peace – a mere ruse in *Ḥamās*' eyes. The mass expulsion was a hard blow for the supporters of the peace negotiations with Israel. In contrast to this, the deportation of *Ḥamās*-followers reinforced the political and moral standing of the Islamic Resistance Movement among the Palestinians in the Territories.

NOTES

1. Unnumbered *Bayān Ḥamās*. In: FM, January 1993, p. 5.
2. Ibid.
3. Memorandum to the Palestinian leadership in Tunis. In: FM, January 1993, p. 21.
4. Ibid.
5. Rabbi Aviner is convinced that "while God requires normal nations to abide by abstract codes of justice and righteousness, such laws do not apply to Jews". In: Ian Lustick, *Middle East International*, no. 471, 18 March 1994, p. 16.
6. See Ali Jarbawi and Roger Heacock, "The Deportations and the Palestinian-Israeli Negotiations". In: *Journal of Palestine Studies*, XXII, no. 3, Spring 1993, pp. 32–45.
7. Ibid, p. 37.
8. Unnumbered *Bayān Ḥamās*. In: FM, January 1993, p. 5.

CHAPTER FOURTEEN

The Surprise: The Declaration of Principles in September 1993

At the end of August 1993, an intensive "back channel diplomacy" between the PLO and the Israeli government was unveiled. It had been carried out totally independently of the official peace process continuing in Washington under US-sponsorship and took the entire world by surprise, including the Palestinian negotiating delegation of the official talks and US-President Bill Clinton. Since January 1993, Israel and the PLO had negotiated secretly under the auspices of the Norwegian foreign minister Johan Holst. On the 10 September, the PLO and the State of Israel recognised each other officially in letters. A "Declaration of Principles on Interim Self-Government Arrangements" (DOP) was signed in the White House on 13 September. It proposed a schedule of negotiations, the first step was the redeployment of Israeli troops from the Gaza Strip and the area around the town of Jericho on the West Bank, formally ending occupation and putting the areas under the administration of the newly created Palestinian National Authority (PNA). These dramatic moves strengthened the PLO's position and legitimacy as representative of the Palestinians at the cost of the groups inside the Territories like *Ḥamās*. By being recognised as partner on the international scene, the PLO formally won the inner-Palestinian competition for representation it has been involved in since the outbreak of the *Intifāḍa*.

This development surprised the whole world, including the Islamists. The events put them into a state of supreme alert. *Ḥamās* firmly rejected the accords and the mutual recognition of the PLO and Israel. The Jewish state and its intentions, as well as the PLO leadership and Yassir Arafat, were being criticised in political, economic and religious terms.

Religiously based arguments were more rare than on other occasions which was probably a reaction to the very concrete, political and economic threat the accords represented for the Islamists; in fact two thirds of the DOP dealt with economic questions. Thus the accord was criticised because it procured a "self-rule under Israeli control on two percent of the Palestinian territory",[1] left *al-Quds* and the settlements to Israel, and furthermore bridges, roads and check-points remained under Zionist security control.[2] The agreement was described as "only another face of occupation".[3] In the eyes of Musa Abu Marzuq, then head of the political bureau of *Ḥamās*,[4] it "legalises the occupation" because it did not call for its end nor the end of the Zionist settlement policy.[5] It was nothing but a "new security belt" for the "Zionist" enemy.[6]

The Israeli will to make peace was questioned. In fact, the Israeli acceptance of the peace treaty was a "conspiracy" to stop the *Intifāḍa*, to prevent any *Jihād*-actions against the occuping power.[7] For this aim the "Zionist entity" might " temporarily renounce its expansionary project of political and economical hegemony over the Arab region";[8] Israel was said to make concessions in order to break the Arab boycott and to establish economic links with the Arab countries.[9] The final goal behind it was the access to the energy sources of the region.[10] *Ḥamās* denounced the injustice that the Arab boycott of the enemy state was coming to an end at a time when the Iraqi, Sudanese and Jordanian people suffered from international boycott and siege.[11] The Arab states, which did not seem to understand these dangers, were called to reject the "Gaza-Jericho First" project, to withdraw from the negotiations and to act in accordance with the "longing of the Muslim people".[12]

The emphasis on the economic aspects and prospects of the treaty showed clearly *Ḥamās*' sense of reality and their imbedding in the present. The book of the Israeli foreign minister at that time, Shimon Peres, *Die Versöhnung* confirmed the supposition that economic aspects played a decisive role on the Israeli side. His repetitive call for a common market in the Middle East, free trade treaties, economic competition and modern marketing must have frightened the Islamists because they knew that the Arab countries and especially the Palestinians were still no "equal partners" – as Peres pretended[13] – for the modern, technologised state of Israel that would unilateraly swamp the Arab markets with its products.

Once again the Islamists were in "good company" with their criticism: the Princeton based Professor Edward Said and Salah Abd al-Shafi, the head of Gaza's Economic Development Group, were two prominent critics of the Oslo agreement among those Palestinian intellectuals that certainly did not have any affinity with *Ḥamās*, but still expressed similar concerns. Abd al-Shafi shared *Ḥamās'* analysis that Israel wanted the Palestinians to act "as a bridge for the Israelis to enter Arab markets. Such integration is the precondition if Israel is to in any way become an economic as much as a military power in the region".[14] He warned that open borders would open the Arab markets for Israel, but not for Palestinians who could not compete with an economy that in terms of GNP was currently ten times its own size. "By accepting Gaza-Jericho First, the PLO has given up any notion of developing a genuinely independent Palestinian economic sector" and "with the Declaration of Principles, we will be working for Israel in Gaza rather than in Tel Aviv, but we will be working for them nonetheless".[15] In his eyes, the relationship of dependency would only be restructured – less via the daily immigration of mass labour into Israel, than by opening up the borders between Israel and the economically weak Palestinian entity on one hand and the "subcontracting between Palestinian capital and sectors of Israeli capital" on the other.[16] The result would be the "absolute incorporation into the Israeli economy."[17] Edward Said characterised the Declaration of Principles as "consolidating Israeli occupation with Palestinian acquiescence"[18] – almost literally the concern voiced by *Ḥamās*-speaker Abu Marzuq. Said demanded that the DOP should be modified on questions like Jerusalem, the settlements, the right of return and reparations.[19] Thus the Islamists' concern with economic consequences of the DOP gave the lie to those critics who pretended that the Islamists were simply backward-minded and propagating utopian ideas. They were analysing the document realistically and objecting to it on political and economical terms – defending, in fact, a mainstream position within the camp of critics of the accords.

Switching back to their other set of discourse, *Ḥamās* left no doubt that from the religious point of view, Israel would never be ready for concessions. The movement talked at length about the "Zionist" position on *al-Quds*. The entire town was considered to be the "eternal capital" of Israel. This was characterised as an "article of creed" (*mawqif 'aqā'idī*) which could never be changed and which was not even questioned by most "pragmatic Zionists".[20] There could not be any concessions about it nor negotiations from a Zionists' position.[21] The best proof of this "truth" was the fact that the Arabs did not succeed in two years of discussion in even putting the subject on the negotiation table.[22] Thus the "continuous fight" between the Islamic *Umma* and the Jews was a historical law which taught everybody that the struggle would only end with the definitive defeat of the Jews, since they did not accept God's choice of the Muslims as his ultimate messengers on earth.[23] The possibility of a conclusion of peace (*sulḥ*) based on Islamic law was invoked, but it was stated that the present peace agreement did not fulfill any of the conditions layed down in Islamic law.[24] Instead, it "renounces our rights and does not realize the slightest of our ambitions".[25] It is interesting to note that amid this criticism in religous terms, the accords were described as a "serious set back and dangerous turn in Palestinian national thought" (*al-fikr al-waṭanī al-filasṭīnī*)[26].

Despite the enormous tragedy which the Washington accords represented for *Ḥamās*, it did not despair. In religious terms, the present "Jewish supremacy" was a "dangerous period of time", but was "limited in time".[27] It would definitively end "when Allah wants it to" and would be followed by the defeat of the Jews whose "existence is limited in time".[28] Therefore, the accords only "delay the liberation" of Palestine for years[29] by "giving Israel the chance to prolong its life for a while."[30] Thus Israel's goal, the creation of "Greater Israel" from the Nile to the Euphrates and the "destruction of the *al-Aqṣā*-mosque and the reconstruction of the Temple",[31] would not be achieved in the long term. Abu Maruq also explained that the failure of the accords was "just a matter of time".[32] They were only based on oral promises from the Zionist side and past experiences had shown that the Israelis are "lying".

Therefore, *Ḥamās* announced that the *Jihād* against the enemy would continue "as long as one day follows the other".[33] This was not a political choice, but a religious duty and therefore cannot be negotiated.[34] *Ḥamās* got support for this attitude by various religious institutions. Its parental organisation, the Muslim Brotherhood in Egypt reminded every male and female Muslim of his or her religious duty to work for the liberation of Palestine which would only be possible through "all forms of *Jihād*".[35] The Association of Religious Sages in Palestine (*rābiṭa u'lema' filasṭīn*), close to *Ḥamās*, explained that the legal aspect of the accords were "vain and abominable" (*bāṭil wa munkār*) and therefore not binding for the Islamic *Umma.*[36]

What did this mean with regard to the nascent Palestinian authority? Arafat and his entourage were this time harshly criticised not only for being alienated from the population in the Territories, but also for acting against the will of huge parts of the PLO itself. "A minority" that ascended to leadership was said to "liquidate" the Palestine question in exchange for "personal gains".[37] *Ḥamās* suggested that the PLO leadership "sold our cause to the Zionists in exchange for millions of dollars".[38] It was said that the accords were signed only a few days after a PLO responsible had declared that his organisation received several million dollars. *Ḥamās* accused Arafat of giving up "part after part" of the Palestinian national institutions in the hope of becoming "village chief of Gaza-Jericho" (*mukhtār*)[39] which meant the "right to rule in the service of the enemy".[40] The "submissive and profit-oriented" leadership of the PLO "sold the whole fatherland for a low price" because it was "tired of fighting".[41] This "treacherous project" was seen to make clear to everybody that Arafat's leadership did not represent the Palestinian people but "only itself".[42]

In this point also, the Islamists' criticism was completely in line with other non-Islamist critics (execpt for the reproach of having been paid to sign). Edward Said suggested that according to sources from the PLO Executive Committee, Arafat only took an interest in the sections of the agreement being negotiated in Oslo which concerned him and his future role.[43] All Arafat wanted, according to Said, was "acceptance" by the Israeli and American side: "They weren't interested in fighting, or being equal, they just wanted the white man to say they were okay." All Arafat got in Said's eyes from the Israelis was a mandate "to enforce what they call their security".[44] His resumé was that the PLO succeeded in "being the first national liberation movement in history to sign an agreement to keep an occupying power in place."[45] He called for a boycott of and non-cooperation with the Palestine National Authority (PNA). "So I think the preeminent responsibility of every Palestinian is not to cooperate with the authority that is a surrogate to the Israeli occupation and an incompetent one at that."[46] Said and *Ḥamās* called for the return to the *Intifāḍa*: Said in the sense that local needs be taken care of by the community in parallel institutions as during the *Intifāḍa*,[47] *Ḥamās* furthermore in terms of military struggle.

In line with their conviction and their political aims, the Islamists seized the occasion to further drive a wedge between the PLO leadership and the Palestinian people. Arafat was condemned for only pursuing his personal interests. Thus there was no more difference between the PLO leadership and the other Arab regimes that were rejected because of their self-enrichment and their neglect of national interests. The supposedly Islamic right for disobedience of an unjust ruler was invoked: "*Ḥamās* will not recognise a leadership that imposes cooperation with the Zionist enemy on our people."[48] The Islamist thinker close to *Ḥamās*, Bassam Jarrar, explained what that meant: *Ḥamās*-would, for example, not accept that the "PLO has the right to lay down conditions about, say, *Ḥamās*' military operations against the occupation".[49] But *Ḥamās* did not draw the ultimate conclusion from the accusations against Arafat, it did not call to topple him and the PLO leadership that negotiated the Accords. On the contrary, *Ḥamās* leaders were eager to explain that the movement wanted to avoid armed conflict with the transitional authority. Aware of the danger of civil war among supporters and opponents of the accords, *Ḥamās* repeated its traditional call for unity among the Palestinians and stated that it is eager to avoid civil war. Arafat and his leadership were made fully responsible for "sewing grains of civil strife (*fitna*) within the community".[50] He was blamed for having fully accepted the "US-Zionist plans" aimed at "gaining time and pushing our people into civil war".[51]

Despite *Ḥamās*' firm rejection of the peace agreement and harsh criticism of the PLO that was going to win limited administrative and executive power when the DOP was implemented, the Islamic Resistance Movement did not pass a certain red line in its relationship with the rival. Even though the future Palestinian authority was said to be illegitimate, *Ḥamās* did not call to depose it and its leader Arafat. But it sent a warning by denouncing Arafat in terms that would be able to revert to the supposedly Islamic right to depose an unjust ruler. For the time being, *Ḥamās* was simply making sure that it was not associated with any of the newly created institutions.

Continuing the analysis in political terms, *Ḥamās* denounced another motive for Arafat's acquiescence to Israeli demands: his fear of the Islamist opposition. The Islamists reproached him for having negotiated the accords with the intention to "oppress the opposition" and "at its forehead *Ḥamās*".[52] This appeared to be the common goal of the new "allies", Arafat and the Zionists.[53] Israel was said to have "succeeded in inciting Arafat's troops against the *Mujāhidūn* and the noble among our people" who they called the "fundamentalist movement" and which they consideed to be the "true danger for their interests in the region".[54] Ending the struggle over Palestine was necessary for them to prevent Islamism from becoming a stronger movement.[55]

The most bitter pill to swallow for the Palestinians engaged in fighting the occupation in the Territories was the fact that their action – which provided the Palestinians with a sense of pride and self-esteem for not only being victims – was so little valued. The "ugly agreement" insulted "your strong *Jihād* and your many sacrifices (...) since the Balfour Declaration".[56] Even during the signing ceremony in the White House in Washington, the humiliation for the fighting Palestinians continued. While Peres and Rabin recalled the wounded and killed Jews from the first to the last one, "Arafat and his crew did not mention the Palestinian martyrs with a single word".[57] The readers of *Filasṭīn al-Muslima* were asked if they saw the "pride of the enemies and the humiliation of our leaders?".[58] But the worst was still to come: he "convicted the *Jihād* of the people by calling it terrorism".[59] Arafat furthermore obeyed the Israeli demands by announcing the change of the passage of the Palestinian National Charter that stipulates the destruction of Israel as the goal of the organisation.

This feeling of continuous humiliation voiced by *Ḥamās* had been extremely widespread among Palestinians.[60] In this issue the Islamists again showed their strong psychological sensitivity. Furthermore, this total devaluation of the Resistance activity within the Territories could not be accepted by *Ḥamās* because it was directed against its constituency in the Territories. Its action and the risks to its members lives during the *Intifāḍa* were apparently made worthless, thus taking away their sense of self-esteem. On the other hand, this manoeuvre jeopardized the importance and the influence of the Islamic Resistance Movement which characterised itself as the driving force of the *Intifāḍa* in delimitation to the PLO. Thus, Arafat's accord with Israel was interpreted in the light of the inner-Palestinian struggle for political power, as a manoeuvre to weaken the Islamist movement, especially *Ḥamās*, that was questioning his authority. Most political observers agreed that Arafat saved his weakened position by signing the DOP.

Thus in the aftermath of the Oslo Accords, *Ḥamās* appeared as a pragmatic political force despite a sometimes flamboyant rhetoric. It accurately analysed in economical and political terms the weak points of the "Gaza and Jericho-First" accords that were raised by many non-Islamist critics in the same manner. *Ḥamās*' insistence on the Jerusalem question might partly be explained by its central importance to Muslims; partly it seems to have been dwelled upon in order to allow *Ḥamās* the use of its religious arguments that were otherwise little help for responding to the very precise threats. Furthermore, the Islamists were aware of the sudden change in the political Palestinian landscape that witnessed a strengthened and internationally recognised PLO. *Ḥamās* was no longer an alternative to the PLO, but became the main opposition force of the new Palestinian National Authority. For these reasons, *Ḥamās* rejected the Accords and announced a continuation and intensification of the *Intifāḍa* whose child the Islamic Resistance Movement was: Armed attacks would remind Israel and the Palestinian Authority that *Ḥamās* could not be passed over in the elaboration of any durable solution. But *Ḥamās* did not follow a course of total obstruction. It issued a warning to the PLO-leadership that it could mobilize its supporters in order to openly fight it and the new authority born out of the "treacherous" accords. But for the time being *Ḥamās* leaders wanted to prevent conflict with the nascent Palestinian Authority. The reason was probably the insight that a majority of Palestinians supported the peace deal at this early stage in the desperate hope that it would somehow better their living conditions.[61]

The crucial question became whether *Ḥamās* would ever renounce violence – a precondition for its integration in any political system. Despite the repeated call for the intensification of the *Intifāḍa* and the assurance that "military action is a permanent strategy that will not change",[62] this might be possible. Marzuq himself explained that "the style, the tactics, the tools and the timing" of *Ḥamās*' action could change depending on the "advantage to be realised".[63] This shows a flexibility in the movement's thought which might even make the abandoning of the armed battle thinkable – if it were in the organisation's interest.

The most impressive confirmation of this attitude was the surprising call of Sheikh Ahmed Yassin for a "truce" (*hodna*) with Israel if Israel withdrew from the Occupied Territories.[64] In a letter smuggled out of prison, he called on *Ḥamās*-members to participate in the elections for a Palestinian administrative council to "oppose" the institution from within.[65] His followers were nevertheless called on to continue their opposition to the accords by "all possible civilised means".[66] The leading spokesman of *Ḥamās*, Muhammad Nazzal, confirmed the authenticity of the letter explaining that a "truce with the enemy is a principle sanctioned by Islamic Law (...)."[67] This did not mean a recognition of the Jews' right to Palestine nor an approval of peace, Nazzal continued.

This apparent about-turn by the leader of the Islamic Resistance Movement proved the flexibility and the pragmatism of the organisation.[68] The movement seemed to admit that with the signing of the Oslo accord a new reality was created which it could not totally deny. The movement apparently wanted to avoid a total exclusion from the political developments despite its continous opposition to the accords. But the Sheikh's formula of opposition with "all possible civilised means" must be interpreted as meaning a possible reduction of violence against Israel. The episode underlined the movement's ability to adapt and its interest in political participation. The explanation that the Islamic Law allows such a "truce" with the enemy under certain circumstances appeared as a mere cover for a volt-face that might be politically in the interest of the movement.

NOTES

1. *Bayān Ḥamās* no. 102. In: FM, October 1993, p. 28.
2. Ibid.
3. Ibid.
4. He had been arrested in New York on 25 July 1995 and was released to Jordan in summer 1997.
5. Interview with Marzuq, p. 11. In: FM, November 1993, p. 11/12.
6. Press conference statement *Ḥamās*, 4/9/1993. In: FM, October 1993, p. 29.
7. *Bayān Ḥamās* no. 102. In: FM October 1993, p. 28.
8. Interview Marzuq. In: FM, November 1993, p. 11.
9. Ibid.
10. Ibid.

11. *Bayān Ḥamās* no. 103. In: FM, November 1993, p. 7.
12. *Bayān Ḥamās* no. 102. In: FM, October 1993, p. 28.
13. Shimon Peres, *Die Aussöhnung*, Berlin 1993, p. 140.
14. Interview with Salah 'Abd al-Shafi, p. 13. In: *Middle East Report*, January–February 1994, p. 11ff.
15. Ibid, pp. 12 and 13.
16. Ibid.
17. Salah 'Abd al-Shafi quoted in Graham Usher, "Gaza: the political economy of autonomy". In: *Middle East International*, no. 467, 21.1.1994.
18. Interview, p. 61. In: *Journal of Palestine Studies*, no 2 (Winter 1995), pp. 60–72.
19. Interview, p. 63 .
20. FM, October 1993, p. 19.
21. Ibid.
22. Ibid.
23. Salah 'Abd al-Fatah al-Khalidi, "Euphrates and Nile are Islamic rivers", p. 55. In: FM, October 1993, p. 55/56. See for more detail of this Islamists' conviction Chapter on *Ḥamās* and the Peace Process of this volume.
24. "Memorandum of *Ḥamās* about its refusal of the self-rule", 1995, p. 1.
25. Ibid.
26. Ibid, introduction.
27. al-Khalidi, see footnote 19.
28. Ibid. As a proof of this "truth of faith" (*ḥaqīqa īmāniyya*) follows the analysis of the Hadith about the Night of Ascension to the seven heavens in which Muhammad saw two hidden rivers representing Paradise and two visible ones: The Nile and the Euphrates. These two rivers and the territory between them have belonged to the Muslims since the beginning of human history to the Day of Judgement – this is clearly indicated by the Hadith. Thus the Muslims will get back control over this territory as soon as they decide to return on God's path.
29. "Memorandum *Ḥamās* on refusal of the self-rule", 1995, p. 37.
30. Ibid, p. 6.
31. Interview with the then Deputy Supreme Guide of the Muslim Brotherhood in Egypt who leads the organisation today, Mustafa Mashur. In: FM, November 1993, p. 30.
32. Interview. In: FM, November 1993, p. 11.
33. *Bayān Ḥamās* no. 103. In: FM, November 1993, p. 7.
34. Ibid.
35. FM, October 1993, p. 41.
36. Interview with the organisation's deputy leader, Sheikh Tamimi. In: FM, October 1993, p. 40. As I have shown previously, the recognition of a dominant position for the Jews contradicts God's turning away from the Jews and His plan to make the Muslims rule on earth; it does not conform to the divine message of Islam and is therefore not binding.
37. *Bayān Ḥamās* no. 102. In: FM, October 1993, p. 28.
38. Ibid.
39. Press conference statement *Ḥamās*, 4.9.1993. In: FM, October 1993, p. 29.

40. *Bayān Ḥamās* no. 103. In: FM, November 1993, p. 7.
41. Press conference statement *Ḥamās*, 4.9.1993. In: FM, October 1993, p. 29.
42. *Bayān Ḥamās* no. 102. In: FM, October 1993, p. 28.
43. Interview with Edward Said, p. 66, in: *Journal of Palestine Studies*, no. 2 (Winter 1995), pp. 60–72.
44. Ibid, p. 67.
45. Ibid, p. 62.
46. Ibid, p. 62.
47. Ibid, p. 63.
48. Interview with Sheikh Sa'ih, in: FM, November 1993, p. 13/14.
49. Ibid, p. 29.
50. *Bayān Ḥamās* no. 102. In: FM, October 1993, p. 28.
51. *Bayān Ḥamās* no. 103. In: FM, November 1993, p. 7.
52. *Bayān Ḥamās* no. 103. In: FM, November 1993, p. 7.
53. Press conference statement *Ḥamās*, 4.9.1993. In: FM, October 1993, p. 29.
54. *Bayān Ḥamās* no. 103. In: FM, November 1993, p. 7.
55. Ibid.
56. *Bayān Ḥamās* no. 102. In: FM, October 1993, p. 28.
57. FM, October 1993, p. 2.
58. Ibid.
59. *Bayān Ḥamās* no. 103. in: FM, November 1993, p. 7.
60. See interview with Edward Said, *Journal of Palestine Studies*, no. 2 (Winter 1995), p. 65. "We have to feel that we are equal. (…) The Israelis are out not only to take everything from us – they already did that – but to humiliate us in the full sense of the word." The psychiatrist, founder of the Gaza Community Mental Health Programme and participant in the Palestinian delegation to the bilateral peace talks, Eyad Elsarraj, states that "there is a growing consensus among the Palestinians that the peace accords have devastated their dream of liberation" and that underneath that mood "lies the feeling of defeat in sharp contrast to the euphoria of victory experienced during the initial stages of the Intifada". In: Eyad Sarraj, "Shaping a culture of peace," p. 59. In: *Palestine-Israel Journal*, Autumn 1994, pp. 57–61.See also Azmy Bishara, Palestinian citizen of Israel, teaching at Bir Zeit University: He tries to show his students "how this agreement does not embody equality." Interview, p. 6. In: *Middle East Report*, January–February 1994, pp. 5–7.
61. Opinion polls show that the DOP received 65 percent of support in September 1993, the Gaza-Jericho-agreement 57 percent in May 1994. Quoted after Khalil Shakaki, The peace process, national reconstruction, and the transition to democracy in Palestine, in: *Journal of Palestine Studies*, Winter 1996 (2), p. 6.
62. Interview with Marzuq. In: FM, June 1994, p. 17
63. Ibid.
64. Letter Yassin. In: *Jerusalem Post*, 3.11.1993, p. 1.
65. Ibid.

66. Ibid.
67. Ibid.
68. *Le Monde Diplomatique* suggests that this is more a sign for the lack of unity of the movement.

CHAPTER FIFTEEN

The Massacre of Hebron, February 1994

On the 25 February 1994, the Israeli settler Baruch Goldstein entered the Ibrahimi mosque in Hebron, which was guarded by Israeli soldiers, and killed 29 Muslims while they were praying at the end of Ramadan. For *Ḥamās*, this massacre was another proof for the evil character and intentions of the "Zionist enemy".

Ḥamās seized this opportunity to explain politics again along religious lines. The massacre was an "expression of the deep hatred of Islam and the Muslims"[1] felt by the Jews and an "open aggression against the Islamic creed and the Muslim culture".[2] While pretending to wish peace, the "Zionist enemy only treats us ruthlessly and wants to weaken us by inflicting wounds so that we surrender to him".[3] The Islamic Resistance Movement understood the killing not as the act of the individual Goldstein, but a "premeditated" (*qad khuṭṭiṭa*) Jewish conspiracy. The massacre was said to have been "planned by the occupation army in cooperation with the settlers" and therefore the "terrorist government of Rabin" is considered a "full participant in the crime".[4] *Ḥamās* refused the apology of the "terrorist Rabin".[5] Consequently, *Ḥamās* insisted on the withdrawl from the negotiations and called on the PLO to return to the armed struggle against Israel

The massacre of Hebron easily confirmed *Ḥamās*' view of the Jews. If Baruch indeed acted on his personal account, the ideology behind the crime was shared by a small group of Israeli extremists organised in the Kach-movement of the late Rabbi Me'ir Kahane, the *Kahane chai* (Kahane lives) and the settler's movement *Gush Emunim*. At Baruch's funeral, his deed was praised as a "selfless act" that had been committed in the interest of the entire Jewish people.[6] In his settlement he was partly praised as a "martyr" and a "hero". Commentaries of extremist rabbis who claimed that "a Jew who kills a non-Jew is exempt from human judgement and has not violated the prohibition of murder"[7] or that "by fighting the Arabs, Israel carries out its divine mission to serve as the heart of the world"[8] only fueled the Islamists' belief in the corrupt and inhuman character of the Jews. This extremist school of thought within Israeli society in fact confirmed the image of the treacherous Jew full of hatred directed against Muslims according to the ancient Islamic traditions. Sheikh Tamimi, deputy president of the Association of the Religious Sages in Palestine close to *Ḥamās*, made the link between both ages by denouncing the Israelis as "murderers of our Prophets and messengers whose hands are soaked with the blood of our best martyrs".[9] *Ḥamās* did not want to distinguish between these groups and the majority of the Israelis and their government; partly because there are links from the political establishment to these extremists; but primarily because the Islamists believed that Israel was a religious state ruled by religious people. Therefore they could easily believe that the above-mentioned views of certain extremist rabbis are representative of the attitude of Israeli society towards the Palestinians and they judged the events as a "confirmation of the impossibility of coexistence between the Palestinian and the Zionist people".[10]

Putting the massacre in the political context, the killing was seen as a "new proof for the falseness (...) of the Oslo and Cairo agreements".[11] Since it occured only little time after the "treacherous Cairo agreement about security questions" it should "open the eyes about the idea of a peace with the enemy".[12] The occupation was described as an "evil disease like cancer" for which there was only one remedy: "extermination" (*isti'ṣāl*).[13]

Ḥamās therefore called the Palestinian people to take their "security and their honour" into their own hands by continuing the *Jihād* and the Resistance. "We must defend ourselves".[14] "Let the massacre be the beginning of a new episode of our *Jihād* and the *Intifāḍa*."[15] This call was supported by the Qur'anic verses: "Make war on them: God will chastise them at your hands and humble them. He will grant you victory over them and heal the spirit of the faithful."[16]

The massacre was definitely a major threat for the peace project negotiated by Arafat and the PLO. *Ḥamās* did not miss its chance to virulently attack those responsibles. "Let us overthrow the symbolic figures of the surrender (...) who are sitting in Tunis looking at the wounds of our people and our *Umma*."[17] "The Oslo faction, the Arafat faction continues in its error and persists in its treachery" – "will this conspiracy continue" was the rhetorical question. The Palestinian and Arab negotiators were called to immediately and definitively withdraw from the negotiations,[18] and the Tunis-leadership was asked to return to the Resistance. *Ḥamās* addressed itself directly to the "brothers" of *Fataḥ* calling them to continue the fight against the occupying army "despite the pressure they are exposed to".[19] The Hebron massacre is presented as a "chance for those who are mistaken to overthrow their calculations and to return to the ranks of the people".[20] The people were said to "ask for revenge" and to choose the Resistance, "an option built up by *Ḥamās*".[21]

It is interesting to note that the *Ḥamās*-activists, despite the increasing violence in its criticism of the PLO and Arafat, were still more cautious than the *Ḥamās*-followers outside the Occupied Territories. In *Filasṭīn al-Muslima*, Arafat was personally made responsible for the course of events: only a guarantee given previously by the Arafat faction not to give up the peace process made such a massacre possible.[22] Therefore, Arafat's leadership was a "participant in the abominable massacre".[23] Arafat's integrity was furthermore questioned: why did he never talk about security for the Palestinians except if there are TV-cameras? Did he "really care about the security of the Palestinians?"[24] The opposition forces within the Territories were called on to "profit from the historical opportunity presented by the Hebron massacre to take over the leadership of the Palestinian people".[25]

The massacre was thus seen as an instruction for the Palestinians who were otherwise "brainwashed" by the Arab state media or the declarations of the PLO. The event should have opened their eyes to the nature of the Jews and the peace treaty and thereby confirmed *Ḥamās'* argumentation. The movement thus seized the opportunity to win wider support among the Palestinians in the struggle for political power. Once again, religious convictions and political motivations and aims were mixed in the skillful way that is characteristic for the Islamic Resistance Movement.

NOTES

1. Press conference statement *Ḥamās*. In: FM, April 1994, p. 25.
2. Ibid.
3. *Bayān Ḥamās* no. 108. In: FM, April 1994, p. 15.
4. Ibid.
5. Ibid.
6. Quoted from *Weltgeschehen*, 1/95, p. 127.
7. Rabbi Israel Ariel. Quotes from *Middle East International*, no. 471, 18 March 1994, p. 16.
8. Rabbi Eliezar Waldman, then a Knesset member and later the director of the main yeshiva in Kiryat Arba. Quoted in *Middle East International*, no. 471, 18 March 1994, p. 17.
9. Statement. In: FM, April 1994, p. 33. For encouragement, he reminds the Palestinians of the Qur'anic verse "Take heart and don't despair. Have faith and you shall triumph." Ibid.
10. FM, April 1994, p. 37.
11. Ibid.
12. *Bayān Ḥamās* no. 108. In: FM, April 1994, p. 15.
13. Press conference statement *Ḥamās*. In: FM, April 1994, p. 25. The truthfulness of this position is proven by the Qur'anic verse 85,8 that is mentioned in the text: "Nor did they torture them for any reason save that they believed in God, the Mighty, the Praised." Ibid.
14. *Bayān Ḥamās* no. 108. In: FM, April 1994, p. 15.
15. Ibid.
16. Qur'an 9,14. Used in press conference statement, in: FM, April 1994, p. 25.
17. *Bayān Ḥamās* no. 108.
18. Unnumbered *Bayān Ḥamās*. In: FM, April 1004, p. 31.
19. Letter reproduced in FM, April 1994, p. 39.
20. Ibid.
21. Unnumbered *Bayān Ḥamās*. In: FM, April 1994, p. 31.
22. FM, April 1994, p. 39.
23. Ibid.
24. Ibid.
25. Ibid, p. 37.

CHAPTER SIXTEEN

Relation between *Ḥamāṣ* and the Palestinian National Authority (PNA)

FIRST PALESTINIAN ELECTIONS JANUARY 1996

In May 1994, after the Israeli troup redeployment, a 10000-men-strong Palestinian police force rolled into Gaza and Jericho. In July 1994, Arafat returned to Palestine at the head of the Palestinian National Authority (PNA). In order to legitimize his rule and the Palestinian representatives for the final status negotiations, the first general elections within the territories of the Palestinian National Authority were scheduled on 15 January 1996. The president of the Palestinian National Authority and the members of the Palestinian Assembly (PA) were to be elected. *Ḥamās* had to respond to the democracy debate in the post-Oslo era and its position towards general elections. In late 1993 and early 1994, the issue was extensively debated within the movement. The source of the election's legitimacy being the Oslo Accords I and II with Israel, most *Ḥamās* leaders opposed the elections: any participation would implicitly recognise the peace agreements. Nevertheless, until the run-up to the elections, *Ḥamās*' position was not univocal, an internal battle between pragmatists and radicalists was going on. The internal debate was illustrated by the cadidatures of several *Ḥamās*-activists that were only cancelled in the last moment after severe criticism from the *Ḥamās*-leadership.

Musa Abu Marzuq from the political department announced early that *Ḥamās* would not participate in any elections linked to the Oslo Accords and that it would boycott all political and administrative institutions created as a consequence of the Agreement.[1] In his view, the text of the accords subjected the Palestinian National Authority to the Zionist occupation.[2] Therefore the proposed elections were not founded on Palestinian legislation, but took place on the order of the "Zionist occupiers".[3] *Ḥamās* wanted to avoid any cooperation with the occupying power, but would still participate in political life through its "presence in society" and the participation of elections for unions, professional bodies and other popular organisations.[4] At the same time, *Ḥamās* officially rejected, in a statement issued in Amman, any participation in the formation of the Palestinian Authority. The movement called instead for support of the "popular Palestinian institutions", mostly created during the *Intifāḍa* in the Territories, instead of giving money and help to the "leadership that does not represent the people".[5] The doyen of the Islamic Resistance Movement, Sheikh Yassin, had a more nuanced view of elections in the autonomous entity: he proposed to participate in elections for a body enjoying truly legislative power (*ḥukm tashrī'ī qānūnī*)[6] because those would be elections for the "leadership of the people" (*lī-qiyādat al sha'b*). On another occasion, Yassin even considered participation in the proposed elections under the condition of a temporary truce (*hudna*) reached with Israel.[7] This truce would be declared unilaterally by *Ḥamās* and would lead to negotiations with Israel. Its aim would be to strengthen the forces of *Jihād*.

The organisation was furthermore worried because the accords did not forsee any representation of the Palestinians living outside the territories under control of the PNA. The Palestinians living in exile or within the bounderies from 1948 will not be represented.[8] Thus Israel would succeed in dividing the Palestinians and their representations.[9] Marzuq feared that the PLO would profit from this by keeping in place the actual PNC while integrating the elected Palestinians from within the Territories.[10] In January 1996 *Filasṭīn al-Muslima* emphasised that it did not reject elections in general, but only rejected the "Oslo elections" that were not representative legislative elections, but an act to endorse the Oslo Accords and the occupation.[11] The elections were called a "carnival" because they were based on "devotion to the false" (*baṭil*) and neglect of the truth (*ḥaqq*).[12]

Ḥamās' leadership rejected the elections for political reasons. It tried to isolate the Palestinian Authority, hoping that it would soon discredit itself through its cooperation with Israel. The boycott of the institutions to be created through the accords had to be understood from this point of view. And as the idea of the creation of a political party associated with *Ḥamās* was dismissed at that point, the movement did not find a credible answer to the contradiction of opposing the peace accords and participating in institutions born out of those. It chose to stick to the rejectionist line thus only delaying an answer to this crucial question.

On the other hand, *Ḥamās* would try to keep control over popular institutions such as charity networks, administrations and unions, which represented its power basis and through which it could uphold its political influence. Confronted with the popular interest and then participation in the elections, *Ḥamās* showed with this twofold position that it did not reject elections in general. The debate illustrated the recognition within *Ḥamās* that it could not simply ignore the existence and evolution of the Palestinian National Authority and the depending national institutions that would slowly take over and control the typical welfare and social services offered by *Ḥamās* in the pre-national phase. Therefore, Sheikh Yassin asked for elections of a legislative body which would then choose a new leadership. He thus confirmed that *Ḥamās* did not refuse the tool of elections and parliamentary institutions as a whole. At this point, *Ḥamās* clearly departed from the teaching of Qutb who had rejected any man-made institution. The religious arguments advanced by Qutb were not mentioned once in this debate. *Ḥamās* thus simply dropped one feature of the Qutbian concept upon which it had dwelt abundantly on other occasions. Wanting to remain a viable player in the political game, *Ḥamās* could not ignore the democracy debate going on in Palestinian society and again proved its ideological flexibility. Thus *Ḥamās* – despite its non-participation in the first general elections – left a security exit open for political participation in future national polls and institutions. The introduction of the notion of a truce with Israel based on Islamic teaching could have even more far-reaching consequences: it could allow the "temporary" participation of *Ḥamās* in Palestinian self-rule institutions and a timely fixed acceptance of peace agreements.

WAVE OF *ḤAMĀS* SUICIDE OPERATIONS IN FEBRUARY/ MARCH 1996

These moments of almost friendly coexistence were forgotten when the issue of armed attacks against Israeli targets, central to *Ḥamās*' political survival, were at stake. In spring 1996 the suicide attacks in Israel were taken up again as a reaction to the killing of Yahyia Ayyash, called "the Engineer" and head of a workshop constructing explosives for suicide operations, by Israeli Secret Service. Almost 60 people died in the two waves of suicide operations that were claimed to have been carried out by Yahyia Ayyash's Disciples, a group related to *Ḥamās*. On 25 February, two suicide bombs exploded in Jerusalem and at a junction near Ashqelon. On 3 and 4 March, two more suicide operations were carried out in Jerusalem and Tel Aviv. The second wave of bombings precipitated an unprecedented military crack-down against *Ḥamās*-members and sympathizers in the West Bank and the Gaza Strip by both Israel and the Palestine National Authority. Arafat outlawed six Palestinian militias, including *Ḥamās*' Izz ad-Din al-Qassam Brigades. Under international and Israeli pressure, he stated that he would "co-operate fully with Israel to wipe out terrorism".[13] An international anti-terror-summit was held in Sharm el Sheikh on 13 March on the initiative of the US-president Bill Clinton uniting 27 nations among whom 13 Arab states. They condemned terrorism and called for the continuation of the peace process.

Arafat and his police and administration were delegitimised and they were reproached for serving Israel's interests, "to proceed in accordance with the desires and interests of the occupying power."[14] The Palestinian police was said to "expose muscles without brain"[15] by doing the dirty work for the Israeli forces that "take a holiday" from their "impossible task of oppressing the people".[16] The Palestinian police "did not refrain from executing the pratical demands advanced by Shimon Peres".[17] The Palestinian forces were said to have arrested more than 600 Palestinians including Imams and to have closed charitable organisations and mosques and even destroyed furniture and windows. *In Filasṭīn al-Muslima* a photo covering half a page showed two Palestinian policemen destroying the door of a health center, the accompanying text said: "New picture of the old occupation...Palestinian police storming health institutions".[18] In another article the question was raised of whether the Palestinian police is really "maintaining security" or a "new terrorist gang"[19] (*'iṣābat irhāb jedīda*)?

Arafat was described as the "big loser in this campaign against *Ḥamās*" because it did not only increase the popular support of the Islamist Resistance Movement, but it also revealed the "truth of the Oslo agreements".[20] The Palestinian Authority was a mere "hostage" (*rahīna*)[21] of the demands of the "occupying power" and "especially its security interests".[22] Arafat was described as a "prisoner" (*asīra*) of his entente with the occupying power that was "controlling" (*mansūr*)[23] him. This prevented any independent relation between the Palestinian Authority and *Ḥamās* – no matter how *Ḥamās* behaved.[24] But Arafat was not only collaborating with Israel, but even with the United States. It was suggested that the US-administration sent the vice-president of the CIA to the region to coordinate the efforts to fight terrorism and the exchange of information between the Palestinian police and the Israeli secret service.[25] The "summit of the peace-makers" in Sharm el-Sheikh was described by *Filasṭīn al-Muslima* as a "mobilisation of the entire world in war against *Ḥamās*" and was said to have led to a legislation "collectively punishing the Palestinians".[26] A group photo of the participating heads of state holding hands was published and commented as showing the "world standing shoulder to shoulder in their fight against *Ḥamās*"[27].

Filasṭīn al-Muslima tried to delegitimise Arafat and his government in political terms, using the powerful argument that he was defending Israel's interests and not those of his own people. The reaction to the bombings was a unique occasion which highlighted the ambiguous position of the PNA as a buffer between Israeli security interests and the Palestinians, especially since Arafat himself had announced that he would "collaborate" with Israel in order to stop the terror. To be seen as an agent of the hated occuping power is the most destructive label a political party can get in a context like Palestine. But as if this was not enough to discredit the political enemy, the super-weapon "collaboration with the United States" was drawn. The mention of the cooperation with the CIA (and the Israeli secret service) had to be understood this way. And the summit in Sharm el Sheikh was presented as a "conspiracy" of the entire world against *Ḥamās* and the Palestinian people.

While Arafat was shaking hands with the heads of state that never defended the Palestinian cause, his police closed down social institutions run by *Ḥamās* and serving the Palestinian people. The beloved feature of *Ḥamās* representing the Palestinian people while Arafat and his administration were defending their own power – which could only be guaranteed by Israel – came to the fore again. Also, the insistence on the "collective punishment" of Palestinians decided by Israel was supposed to illustrate the symbiosis of *Ḥamās* and the Palestinian people. Furthermore, Israel's collective punishments had always been exploited by *Ḥamās* to win support for its rejectionism at the expense of the conciliatory line of the PLO. To provoke these collective sanctions against Palestinians was probably even one of the aims of *Ḥamās* bomb attacks against Israelis.[28] Still it has to be noticed that the language of *Ḥamās* was not violent, but rational and that there was no use of Islamic symbols or justifications for the criticism. The reaction was also tame in the sense that *Ḥamās* did not call to topple Arafat and his government. *Ḥamās* was playing its role as an opposition force using the armed attacks to highlight and exploit the difficult situation its political enemy Arafat put himself in with the peace-agreements: building a Palestinian sovereignty by serving Israel's interests.

DEATH OF PRISONER IN PALESTINIAN PRISON AND CLASHES BETWEEN PALESTINIAN POLICE AND POPULATION, JULY/AUGUST 1996

The political exploitation of armed attacks followed by the ritual closing down of the Occupied and Autonomous Territories was always a difficult balance to keep. The support of the armed struggle among Palestinians was varying, whereas the approval even by the non-Islamic opposition was unanimous when *Ḥamās* denounced the democratic deficiencies of the PNA. The political prisoner Mahmud Jumayl died on 29 July obviously after having been tortured in a Palestinian prison. Thousands attended his funeral on 1 August in Nablus where youths stoned the municipality buildings. On 2 August, hundreds of Palestinians gathered outside the Tulkarm prison protesting against the detention without trial of several Palestinians. Inexplicably, the police opened fire leaving one Palestinian dead and seven wounded. Both protest gatherings were claimed by *Ḥamās*, even though that in Nablus was led by Fataḥ members.

In a memorandum *Ḥamās* pejoratively called the Palestinian Authority the "Oslo power" (*sulṭa Oslo*)[29] and lamented the "acts of piracy of power" (*qarṣana as-sulṭa*). It took the latest events as a chance to criticise Arafat's human rights violations. "Silencing the citizens by arresting journalists and human rights activists" as well as the "awful torture of more than 100 prisoners" were mentioned as examples of the oppressive politics of the Palestinian Authority. *Ḥamās* warned of the danger of a further fractioning of Palestinian society and explained that it had remained silent for so long in order to maintain unity. But with the two street demonstrations, the "Palestinian people pushed the matter almost to an uprising" (*as scha'b al falesṭīnī qad dafa' al amr ilāhad al-iḥtiqān aladhī yawshuku 'ala al infijār*). Now *Ḥamās* could no longer remain silent in front of torture and oppression and considered it "as its duty to stir up the public in order to stop these practises and to prevent Palestinian society from sliding into the hell of internal clash or a life in the shadow of dictatorship". It called the population to struggle for the "respect of human rights" and the "freedom and glory of the Palestinian people". In a more concrete way, it called the Palestinians to make efforts to stop any financial support of the PNA as the money would only be used to "oppress the people" and asked to "tear away the cover from this power" that did not change its "arrogant manners" nor did it stop playing "the occupier's agent" (*wakīl al-iḥtilāl*).

Filasṭīn al-Muslima published on its back cover the photos of two killed Palestinians as well as a picture of the tortured body. The text simply said: "The murderer was not the occupying power".[30] The situation in Palestinian prisons was described to "not differ a lot" from the one in Israeli prisons.[31] A report of Amnesty International (AI) was used as a source for this statement. *Filasṭīn al-Muslima* took stock of two years of Palestinian National Authority in office: more than 1000 Palestinians were in prison and nine died after torture – "because of their opposition to the Oslo-project and to the government".[32] The "obvious violation of human rights" by the PNA and the restrictions of the freedom of Palestinians were criticised, as well as the fact that nobody was ever held responsible for these transgressions. The "essential task" of the various security services created by Arafat was "the protection of the occupation" (*ḥirāsa al-iḥtilāl*).

Ḥamās was continuing to denounce the subservient attitude of Arafat and his government towards the Israeli occupyers. The lack of progress in the negotiations since the election of the Likud-prime-minister Benjamin Netanjahu in May 1996 made this easy. The criticism was voiced in political terms and psychological ones: the "glory" of the Palestinian people was seen to be threatened by Arafat's politics. The lack of freedom and democracy was denounced and Arafat's rule was described as "dictatorship". Here again, *Ḥamās* joined the broad chorus of non-Islamic political opposition to Arafat that was constantly condemning Arafat's self-satisfied, undemocratic behaviour.[33] The fact that *Filasṭīn al-Muslima* used a report of Amnesty International as a source for their torture-allegations shows the closeness between both discourses in this point. Still, the understanding of freedom of expression and democracy by both groups was certainly different: by emphasising that most of the political prisoners and tortured people were members of Islamist groups, *Ḥamās* clearly called for freedom for these people; whether it would have done so for their political enemies is far from evident.

Despite bitter criticism of the PNA, *Ḥamās* did not openly call for violent opposition or the overthrow of Arafat. It stated that the "people" were about to start a popular uprising this time against Arafat and the abuses of his administration. *Ḥamās* proposed various concrete, but non-violent measures to harm the PNA. It demanded that Palestinians stopped financing it and attempted to uncover its true nature, that of an "agent of the occupying power". *Ḥamās* was conscious of Arafat's attempts to solidify his power base by incorporating the *shabāb*, the youth that led the *Intifāḍa* and *de facto* morally and physically controlled Palestinian society during the uprising. He did this by offering them jobs, mainly in his various police services, which were paid largely by the international aid transferred to Palestine. In its call for non-violent obstruction, *Ḥamās* departed from the methods used by Islamist groups in other Arab countries where authoritarian governments oppressing the people were condemned irrevocably for having turned away from Islam and were asked to be overthrown. This further illustrates the pragmatic attitude of *Ḥamās* that tried to slowly erode the acceptance of the Palestinian Authority knowing that the lack of progress in the peace negotiations played into its hands. Again it looks as though *Ḥamās* played on time and had hoped to participate in or take over the government in the medium run. Certainly, it did not judge this development impossible as their brothers in other Muslim countries do who only believe in violence reflecting the uncompromising attitude of the government towards them. But in case of growing popular discontent and the multiplication of mass demonstrations against the PNA, *Ḥamās* would not hesitate to take over the leadership of such an uprising – even though it will not call for it. This tactic was applied after the outbreak of the first *Intifāḍa* and is completely in line with *Ḥamās*' claim to speak for the people in contrast to the PLO in former times and the PNA today. Thus *Ḥamās* leaves itself another security exit open, the one of the return to a popular uprising against Israel and this time also against Arafat and the official Palestinian leadership.

NOTES

1. Interview with Marzuq. In: FM, November 1993, p. 11.
2. Another interview with Marzuq. In: FM, June 1994, p. 17.
3. Ibid.
4. Ibid.
5. *Bayān Ḥamās* no. 103. In: FM, November 1993, p. 7.
6. FM, November 1993, p. 5.
7. "Letters from Sheikh Yassin", in: *al-Wasat*, 6.11.1993.
8. FM, January 1996, p. 7.
9. Ibid.
10. FM, June 1994, p. 17.
11. FM, January 1996, p. 7.
12. Ibid.
13. *Middle East International*, 15 March 1996, p. 4.
14. FM, April 1996, p. 11.
15. Ibid. Title of the article.
16. Ibid.
17. Ibid, p. 12.
18. Ibid.
19. FM, April 1996, p. 18.
20. FM, April 1996, p. 12.
21. FM, April 1996, p. 18.
22. Ibid.
23. Ibid.
24. Ibid.

25. See FM, April 1996, p. 12.
26. FM, April 1996, p. 20.
27. Ibid.
28. *Ḥamās* explains that it leads a "specific Jihad" that "weakened the strength and capacity of the Palestinian Authority". In: *Memorandum of Ḥamās on the refusal of the self-rule*, 1995, p. 34.
29. Memorandum Hamas, in: FM, September 1996, p. 9. The following quotes are taken from this memorandum.
30. FM, September 1996.
31. FM, January 1997, p. 3
32. FM, September 1996, p. 3.The following quotes are taken from this article.
33. The hurting comparison between torture in Palestinian and Israeli prisons was also advanced by Fataḥ-activists. See *Middle East International*, no. 532, 16 August 1996, p. 10.

CHAPTER SEVENTEEN

Outlook

In the present transitional phase of Palestinian politics in which the peace process and the Palestinian national state-building could continue, but a return to open warfare between Israel and Palestinians cannot totally be excluded, *Ḥamās* offers a programme corresponding in its indecision to the open situation. On one hand, it is sticking to the ideology developed and proved to be worthwile during the *Intifāḍa*, rejecting the peace agreements and calling for the continuation of the *Intifāḍa* against Israel in order to liberate the entire territory of Palestine. On the other hand, it was forced to take notice of the decisive changes that have occured since the Oslo accords, primarily the installation of a central Palestinian power collaborating with Israel in the autonomous territories. It thus took a stance on issues of the state-building process like elections and democracy. Clearly, *Ḥamās* does not accept the monopoly of violence of the new central power, it continues the armed attacks against Israeli targets whenever it judges this to be opportune. Conscious of the realities on the ground and the popular support for the nascent government, it seems to have accepted the existence of the PNA; it does not call to fight it, but waits for its self-destruction from compromising too much with Israel. It continues to work in local politics by participating in elections for unions, chambers of trade, universities. Despite the fact that *Ḥamās* in the end did not participate in the general elections for institutions created on the basis of the rejected peace accords with Israel, *Ḥamās* has left the ideological door open for a participation in the future. If the peace process is to continue and the competences of the Palestinian administration are to be widened, *Ḥamās* might decide to create or become a political party in order to participate further in the political scene. The justification for such a turn-about would probably be to serve the interests of the Palestinian people as we have seen several times before. The temporary measure of a truce supposedly based on Islamic teaching, as proposed by Sheikh Yassin in the context of the elections, allowing *Ḥamās* to participate in institutional life despite its rejection of Israel, gives an indication of the manner in which this choice could be presented to the movement's constituency. But as long as there is a chance that the peace process might come to an end – and this danger seems strong in April 1997 – *Ḥamās* cannot fully chose this path. On the contrary, it has to make sure that it remains the leading force of an eventual new *Intifāḍa* against Israel. Why should the movement give up its rejectionist programme at a time when even Palestinians involved in the self-rule do not exclude the outbreak of a warfare as a consequence of the continuous provocation and humiliations from the Israeli president Netanjahu and the Likud government? The Palestinians and *Ḥamās* know that Israel is always militarily superior, but with the weapons present in the Autonomous Territories, the Palestinians could do a lot of harm to Israel whose public is probably not ready to accept the death of Israeli soldiers. In this scenario, Israeli public opinion could end the warfare by pressure on its own government like in the war in Lebanon. Thus the repetitive call for *Jihād* in the form of armed struggle against Israel is not completely unworldly and out of touch with the political development as it might seem at first glance. If things turn out to move in the opposite direction, *Ḥamās* could reinterpret the notion of *Jihād*, giving it a more reformist meaning.

We find the same openness in relation to Arafat and the Palestinian National Authority. On one level there is a sort of coexistence: *Ḥamās* plays the political opposition criticising the undemocratic, authoritarian character of Arafat's rule more and more resembling the one-party-rule established in other Arab countries, denouncing torture, corruption and the increasing patronage-system thus reflecting strong concern in Palestinian society. If in addition the economic situation further deteriorates, *Ḥamās* could become the exclusive representative of the "underdogs" of Palestinian society. The peace accords did not bring the anticipated improvement of the precarious economic situation of the Palestinian society. On the contrary, the frequent closures of the Territories since then lead to an unprecedented rise in unemployment and an impoverishment of the Palestinians.[1] In the Autonomous Territories, most jobs have been created in non-productive sectors like the PNA-administration and the various police forces. Arafat's loyalists have been attributed monopolies for importing strategic products such as petrol, construction materials and cigarettes, often in close collaboration with Israeli enterprises. The private sector – the engine of any lasting economic developement – has been totally neglected. Thus the economic dependence on Israel is continuing, if not growing, and Arafat's use of the limitations of economic development imposed by Israel in order to extend his control to Palestinan economy is increasingly angering the Palestinians. If the nascent economic disparity between those close and loyal to Arafat and the other Palestinians is going to develop further, *Ḥamās* could become the representative of the unprivileged of Palestinian society and those merchants whose economic aspirations are being disappointed. The strong social components in *Ḥamās*' discourse and work and the supposedly religiously based call for equality would qualify the movement for such a role. If popular support would turn away from the central power for these reasons, *Ḥamās* could fall back upon the notion of *Jahiliyya* as interpreted by Qutb and his successors, meaning the revolt against its own Muslim rulers with the argument that they have deviated from the right path. *Ḥamās* has already issued warnings in this sense, but until now judged it more opportune to not cross this line. The sudden death of Arafat, whose successor will never enjoy the same authority and popular confidence, could be the moment judged convenient by *Ḥamās* for taking up the more confrontational elements that its ideology offers for the inner-Palestinian struggle.

NOTES

1. See Sara Roy, "Alienation or Accomodation?", *Journal of Palestine Studies*, no. 4 (Summer 1995), pp. 73–82 for a grim vision of the Palestinian future based on the economic and social de-development since the Oslo Accords.

Chapter Eighteen

Conclusion

The Muslims' thought and teaching "has to be purged from the effects of intellectual assault".[1] In the eyes of *Ḥamās*-activists, the elimination of foreign intellectual influences from Muslims' hearts and minds is the precondition for any change of the wretched situation the Arab-Muslim countries and the Palestinians find themselves in. The return to a supposedly purely Islamic system of thought is the only way to strengthen the Islamic *Umma*; because only a nation whose thought is undermined by alien influences can be defeated militarily.[2]

The Islamists – consciously or unconsciously – do not want to acknowledge that it became virtually impossible to isolate systems of thought in our contemporary world: mass media spread news in seconds all over the globe, world-wide trade networks and inter-global connections in other domains make constant contact and exchange possible and necessary. The dominance of Western technology, economy and thought makes the independent development of other systems of thought difficult. At least, they can often be described as responses to Western ideas, threats and criticisms. The ideology of *Ḥamās* is the best proof for this: it is far from being static or simply reverting to an ancient Islamic model. It can rather be characterized as based on traditional Islamic teaching, enriched with modern concepts and ideas of mainly Western origin. Even the aspects of traditional Islamic teaching in *Ḥamās*' system of thought are often influenced by non-Islamic concepts; in their application to contemporary situations and problems, the interpretation and emphasis of such elements of traditional Islamic teaching often change. Thus the conviction that the Islamic *Umma* is the "best nation" is transformed into an appeal to Arab-Muslim governments to defend the Palestinians' interests in the international arena by means of modern politics like economic boycotts and state interventions. In the call for *Jihād*, the emphasis is shifted from the community to the individual. Appeals are directed to the consciousness of the individual believer – according to the central place the individual occupies in modern contemporary societies and politics.

Furthermore, we have seen the Western ideas of the nation-state and of nationalism integrated into *Ḥamās*' system of thought. The call for democracy and a multi-party system, as well as the insistence on the will of the people as supreme authority are obviously borrowed from Western liberal thought; elements of Christian anti-Semitism found their way into the Islamists' image of the Jew as well. Another source of borrowing is Judaism: the idea of the sanctity of the Palestinian territory seems clearly to have been taken over from the enemy's doctrine. In Islamic teaching, territory is important in the sense that God's rule over it should be secured. But except the towns of Mekka and Medina and their immediate surroundings, no territory has a more central place than another in Islamic teaching.

The methods of absorption of these "alien" ideas and concepts vary. The ideas seem mainly to be assimilated through a process of Islamisation. A single idea is claimed to be of purely Islamic origin, such as nationalism, which is simply declared part of the Islamic creed; or the entire Western civilization is classified as a mere prolongation of an original Islamic civilisation. Thus the principles of the French Revolution, *liberté, egalité* and *fraternité* can be declared Islamic values without any further theoretical elaboration. The method of Islamisation goes back to the Qur'ān itself: Islam considers the Torah, the Gospels and the Qur'ān as different expressions of the same, unique godly revelation. Abraham, who established the doctrine of monotheism, was the first Muslim and true believer, but his descendants neglected their scripture and God therefore sent his message again in form of the Christian and later Islamic revelation. Islam thus had existed from all eternity. This doctrine results in an Islamisation of all history before Muhammad. The Islamists apply the same technique today, which allows them to integrate non-Islamic ideas without acknowledging their foreign origin. This procedure allows a society on the defensive, such as the Arab-Muslim society, to borrow from outside without losing its vigorously defended self-esteem and self-assertion.

Nevertheless, the Islamists seem to be aware of the decisive role the West plays in today's world. This awareness and a deep knowledge of Western ideas and patterns of reactions becomes obvious in the Islamists' effort to explain and justify their cause and action, not only according to Arab-Islamic criteria, but also according to the Western yardstick. In order to mobilize Palestinians and other Muslim Arabs in the struggle against Israel, *Ḥamās* emphasizes that its *Jihād* respects the rules of the classical Islamic *Jihād*-doctrine. Thus every Muslim should feel compelled to participate. At the same time, the Islamists know that the notion of *Jihād* only raises fear and incomprehension in the West so they present their armed struggle as a liberation war to the Western audience, comparing it to the Jewish resistance against the British Mandate forces. In this new light, the Palestinians' struggle becomes legitimized according to Western standards.

Another example of the explanation according to a double yardstick can be observed in the question of the Palestinian Christians. They are assured of being respected as a religious minority (*ahl al-kitāb*) according to Islamic teaching. The precondition is, however, the recognition of the superiority of Islam. The West, on the other hand, is reassured in a different way about the fate of the Christians in an Islamic state: the Islamists invoke the "most basic idea" of democracy which states that a minority has to accept the rule of the majority. This is simply the case of the Christian minority, which has to accede to the will of a Muslim majority. Any possible criticism from Western liberal thinkers concerning the treatment of Christians in an Islamic state is thus repelled by the very ideas of Western liberalism.

All these examples show the deep intrusion of foreign and often Western ideas into contemporary fundamentalist Islamic thought. Reaction to Western ideas, threats or criticism can be often detected as the motivating force behind the system of thought of *Ḥamās*. This characteristic puts the ideology of *Ḥamās* in a historical line with earlier Islamic thought in this century.

One of the most striking features of *Ḥamās*' reaction to the peace process is nevertheless that it is often in line with prominent critics of the Accords belonging to the secular opposition. As shown previously, the rejection of the peace accords on the basis of religious arguments is only one pillar of the argument; the other is a political and economical analysis that overlaps with critcism pronounced by prominent intellectuals from the secular camp like Edward Said or Salah Abd al-Shafi. There is even concord in the means they propose to oppose the deal: Said and *Ḥamās* call for a continuation of the *Intifāḍa* – Said means this in the sense that the parallel institutions created during the *Intifāḍa* should remain at work, *Ḥamās* adds to this concept the interpretation of *Jihād* as a military struggle. Again, on the question of the undemocratic character of Palestinian national institutions and Arafat's authoritarian and high-handed style, *Ḥamās* joins a broad chorus of critics. The fact that the Islamist movement frequently voices almost mainstream concerns shows its closeness to the society, its realism and its capacity to further develop its position as a major political force.

I would in fact argue that *Ḥamās*' ideology has corresponded and still corresponds extremely well to the concrete needs and aspirations of the Palestinians living inside the Occupied and Autonomous Territories. The Islamists' discourse of social justice responds to the despair of the Palestinians about the disastrous economic situation and the lack of economic development in the Territories before and since the peace-accords. The identity crisis, faced by any society in the modernization process, but in this case particularly aggravated by the constant Israeli denial of Palestinian identity, is counterbalanced by the strong cultural assertion and the insistence on Islamic values. The need for solidarity finds its ideological expression in the Islamic call for solidarity among believers. The dichotomous Qur'ānic teaching, describing *ḥaqq* and *bāṭil* as two totally separate categories, can easily be applied to an armed struggle between two parties over territory in which the interests of oneself and the enemy seem absolutely incompatible. The daily humiliation suffered by most Palestinians, and especially by those wage workers who cross daily the Green line into Israel, created a ground on which *Ḥamās*' defamation and demonization of the Jews can flourish. The call for democratization corresponded to the popular nature of the *Intifāḍa* and the mass-based institutional life inside the Territories, assuring a participation of the majority of the population. Thus the ideology of *Ḥamās* seemed to be capable of channelling all sorts of opposition to the status quo.

It is nevertheless true that the granting of autonomy to parts of the Territories, the election of Arafat as president of the newly created

Palestinian National Authority (PNA) and the creation of a Palestinian police force have radically changed the political situation. It first looked as though peace agreement – initially supported by 64.9 percent of the Palestinians in the hope for better living conditions and more freedom[3] – would assure the political victory of the PLO over the rejectionist *Ḥamās* that seemed to be out of touch with the events. But initial hopes in the peace process were soon disappointed by Israel's continuous occupation and violation of the interim agreement, by the mismanagement of the PNA and its oppressive methods and the massive decline in the already poor economic situation due to the frequent closure of the West Bank and the Gaza Strip. One observer states that "there is a sense of the end of the dream, something Palestinians have never before contemplated".[4] This widespread deception plays in to the hands of the oppositional *Ḥamās* which rejects the peace agreement and its conditions. Thus the spokesman of *Ḥamās* in Gaza, Mahmud Zahhar, can confidently declare that "*Ḥamās* is not in a hurry", knowing that "the PLO's practise will inevitably lead to its downfall".[5] Meanwhile, *Ḥamās* continues to spread its message and world view through its network of charity and social institutions, through the Islamic university in Gaza and the various chambers of commerce, municipalities and trade unions where it often holds a majority of seats. The peace agreement certainly destabilized the movement and forced it to respond to challenges like the democracy debate and the election issue; the controversial debate about the use of suicide attacks shows the deep trenches separating the various wings within the movement. Still, astonishingly enough, *Ḥamās* did not have to significantly alter its message since Israel and the PLO signed the peace accords; its confrontational discourse still applies to the relations full of tension and hatred between Israel and the Palestinians and the conflict between "those from Tunis" and "those who remained" continues within the Autonomous Territories. Nevertheless, the state-building process in Palestine requires a different argument than the struggle against a common enemy and this is expressed mainly in the shift of emphasis between the supposedly religious discourse on one hand and the political and economical one on the other hand: the religious rhetoric dominates in questions like Jerusalem or access to the Ibrahimi mosque in Hebron where little flexibility can be detected until now; on other subjects like general elections or torture in Palestinan prisons, there is little place for religious arguments, they are addressed in mainly political terms.

The enormous margin between *Ḥamās*' oral denunciations and its "Realpolitik" thus justifies optimism about the future. The ideological flexibility and pragmatism of the movement could allow *Ḥamās* to find a way of participating in the structures and institutions related to the autonomy status – if this were in its political and strategic interest. The non-participation in the elections was a political decision taken after long discussions, not a matter of faith. It became clear that *Ḥamās* does not reject the idea of elections as the way to chose a popular leadership. *Ḥamās* thus has the potential to become a political party. It is true, however, that in the long-term perspective, the flexible and pragmatic nature of fundamentalist thought could prove to be a weakness. The fixed principles of traditional Islamic thought could be eroded by the absorption of too many "alien" concepts, increasing the inner contradictions of the Islamists' ideology. Superficially adapted ideas, like the call for democracy, are restricted by other major pillars of their system of thought, such as the condition of religious minorities.

While the beginning of the state-building process led to a decline in popular support of political violence as perpetrated by *Ḥamās*, the continuous provocations of the new Israeli president Netanjahu and the Likud government could lead to a collective despair and a Palestinian environment which again generates mass support for violence and thus strengthens *Ḥamās* at the expense of the secular-nationalist forces. With the perspective of a return to an *Intifāḍa*-like situation and as long as an independent Palestinian state lies in such an uncertain future, the Islamic Resistance Movement can stick successfully to large parts of the ideology and intellectual mechanisms developed during the *Intifāḍa*.

NOTES

1. *Mīthāq*, p. 17: "*takhallus (manāhij al-ta'līm) min athār al-ghazū al-fikrī* (...)."
2. Ibid. The crusaders had already understood this simple truth and thus prepared their military attack by infiltrating Islamic thought with their ideas. Ibid.

3. See the opinion poll conducted by the Center for Palestine Studies and Research (CPRS) on 10/11.9.1993, two days before the declaration of principles was signed.
4. Sara Roy, "Alienation or Accommodation?", p. 80, in: *Journal of Palestine Studies*, no. 4, Summer 1995, pp. 73–82.
5. Interview, p. 83, in: *Journal of Palestine Studies*, no. 3, Spring 1995, pp. 81–88.

Bibliography

Abed, George, T., "The Political Economy of Resistance in the Occupied Territories". In: *Journal of Refugee Studies* (1989), pp. 55–64.

Abu-Amr, Ziad, "Class Structure and the Political Elite in the Gaza Strip: 1948–1988". In: Aruri, *Occupation*, pp. 77–98.

Abu-Amr, Ziad, "The Politics of the Intifada". In: Hudson (ed), *Palestinians*, pp. 3–24.

Abu-Amr, Ziad, *Al-Ḥarakāt al-Islāmiyya fī l-Ḍiffa al-Gharbiyya wa Qiṭā'* Ghazza, ('Akkā, 1989).

Abu-Amr, Ziad, *Islamic Fundamentalism in the West Bank and Gaza: Muslim Brotherhood and Islamic Jihad*, (Bloomington, Indiana University Press, 1994).

Abu-Amr, Ziad, "Hamas: A historical and political background". In: *Journal of Palestine Studies*, no. 4, (Autumn 1991), pp. 5–19.

Ajami, Fouad, *The Arab Predicament. Arab Political Thought and Practice Since 1967*, (Cambridge, 1981).

Ahmed, Hisham H., *Hamas. From Religious Salvation to Political Transformation: The Rise of Hamas in Palestinian Society*, (Jerusalem, 1994).

Ali, Ameer, *The Spirit of Islam. A History of the Evolution and Ideals of Islam*, (London, 1922).

Aruri, Naseer (ed), *Occupation. Israel over Palestine*, 2nd ed, (Belmont, 1989).

al-Ashmawy, Muhammad Said, *L'Islamisme contre l'Islam*, (Paris, 1989).

Ashrawi, Hanan Mikhail, "The Politics of Cultural Revival". In: Hudson (ed), *The Palestinians*, pp. 77–87.

Awartani, Hisham, "Obstacles to Opportunity". In: *Journal of Refugee Studies* (1989), pp. 64–70.

Ayubi, Nazih N., *Political Islam. Religion and Politics in the Arab World*, (London/New York, 1991).

Azzam, Maha, "Islamist Attitudes to the Current World Order". In: *Islam & Christian-Muslim Relations*, 4iii (1993), pp. 247–256.

al-Azmeh, Aziz, "Arab Nationalism and Islamism". In: *Review of Middle East Studies*, 4 (1988), pp. 33–51.

Barghouti, Mustafa, "Popular/Mass Movement in the Community", p. 125. In: *Journal of Refugee Studies* (1989), pp. 125–131.

Baron, Xavier, *Les Palestiniens. Un Peuple*, (Paris, 1984).

Benvenisti, Meron, *The West Bank Data Project. Demographic, economic, legal, social and political developments in the West Bank*, (Boulder, 1987). Referred to as WBDP.

Carré, Olivier, *Mystique et Politique. Lecture Revolutionaire du Coran par Sayyid Qutb, Frère Musulman Radical*, (Paris, 1984).
Choueiri, Youssef M., *Islamic Fundamentalism*, (London, 1990).
Choueiri, Youssef M., "Neo-Orientalism and Islamic Fundamentalism". In: *Review of Middle East Studies*, (4) 1988, pp. 52–68.
Cohn, Norman, *Warrant for Genocide. The Myth of the Jewish World-Conspiracy and the Protocols of the Elders of Zion*, (London,1967).
Enayat, Hamid, *Modern Islamic Political Thought. The Response of the Shi' and Sunni Muslims to the Twentieth Century*, (London, 1982).
Ende, Werner und Steinbach, Udo (eds), *Der Islam in der Gegenwart*, (München, 1984).
Etienne, Bruno, *L'Islamisme Radical*, (Paris, 1987).
Ernst, Friedhelm, "Problems of UNRWA School Education and Vocational Training". In: *Journal of Refugee Studies* (1989), pp. 88–98.
Esposito, John (ed), *Voices of Resurgent Islam*, (Oxford, 1983).
Fasheh, Munir, "Education under Occupation". In: Aruri, *Occupation*, pp. 511–535.
Frisch, Hillel, "The Case of Religious Emulation: The Nationalization of Universal Religious Doctrine in the Palestinian Fundamentalist Movement. In: *Middle East Focus*, vol. 13 (3),1990, pp. 18–25.
Gibb, H.A.R. and Brown (eds), *Islamic Society and the West*, (London,1950).
Graham-Brown, Sarah, "The Economic Consequences of the Occupation". In: Aruri, *Occupation*, pp. 297–360.
Graham-Brown, Sarah, "Impact on the Social Structure of Palestinian Society", p. 380. In: Aruri, *Occupation*, pp. 361–397.
Guillaume, A., *The Life of Muḥammad. A Translation of Ibn Isḥāq's Sīrat Rasūl Allāh*, (London, 1955).
Haddad, Yvonne Yazbeck, *Contemporary Islam and the Challenges of History*, (Albany, 1982).
Haddad, Yvonne Yazbeck, "Sayyid Qutb: Ideologue of Islamic Revival". In: Esposito (ed), *Voices*, pp. 67–98.
Harkabi, Y., *Arab Attitudes to Israel*, (London, 1972).
Hilal, Jamil, "PLO Institutions: The Challenge Ahead". In: *Journal of Palestine Studies*, no. 1, (Autumn 1993), pp. 46–60.
Hillenkamp, Bernard, *Ḥamās: Der historische und soziale Kontext einer Islamistischen Bewegung. Perioden, Entwicklungen und Besonderheiten im Ringen um das "Heilige Land"*, (unpublished master-thesis, Freie Universität Berlin, 1997)
Hodgson, Marshall G.S., *The Venture of Islam. Conscience and History in a World Civilization*, Vol. I, (Chicago, 1974).
Hudson, Michael, C. (ed), *The Palestinians: New Directions*, (Washington, 1990).
Izutsu, T., *Ethnico-Religious Concepts in the Qur'an*, (Montreal, 1966).
Izutsu, T., *God and Man in the Koran. Semantics in the Koranic Weltanschauung*, (Tokyo, 1964).
Al-Jarbawi, 'Ali and Heacock, Roger, "The Deportations and the Palestinian-Israeli Negotiations". In: *Journal of Palestine Studies*, no. 3 (Spring 1993), pp. 32–45.

Al-Jarbawi,'Ali, "The Position of Palestinian Islamists on the Palestine Accord". In: *The Muslim World*, no. 1–2 (January–April 1994), pp. 127–154.

Johnson, Nels, *Islam and the Politics of Meaning in Palestinian Nationalism*, (London, 1982).

Journal of Refugee Studies, (Special Issue: Palestinian Refugees and Non-Refugees in the West Bank and Gaza Strip), Vol. 2, No. 1, (Oxford,1989).

Kepel, Gilles, *Le Prophète et le Pharaon. Les Movements Islamiques dans l'Egypte Contemporaine*,(Paris, 1984).

Kepel, Gilles and Richard, Yann (eds), *Intellectuels et Militants de l'Islam Contemporain*, (Paris, 1990).

Khadduri, Majid, *War and Peace in the Law of Islam*, (Baltimore, 1955).

Khatib, M.M., *The Bounteous Koran. A Translation of Meaning and Commentary*, (London, 1986).

Lapidus, Ira, "The Separation of State and Religion in the Development of Early Muslim Society". In: *International Journal of Middle East Studies*, 6 (1975), pp. 363–385.

Legrain, Jean-Francois, "A Defining Moment: Palestinian Islamic Fundamentalism". In: Piscatori, *Islamic Fundamentalisms in the Gulf Crisis*, (Chicago, 1991), pp. 131–153

Laroui, Abdallah, *Islam et Modernité*, (Paris, 1987).

Lewis, Bernard, *Semites and Anti-Semites. An Inquiry into Conflict and Prejudice*, (London, 1986).

Lockman, Zachary and Beneinin, Joel (eds), *Intifada. The Palestinian Uprising against Israeli Occupation*, (Boston, 1989).

Mattar, Philip, "The PLO and the Gulf Crisis". In: *Middle East Journal*, 46, no. 1 (Winter 1994), pp. 31–45.

al-Mawdudi, Abul A'la, *Tafhīm al-Qur'ān*, six volumes, published 1950–1973. (The first three volumes exist now in English translation: *Towards Understanding the Qur'an*, Leicester, 1988,1989,1990).

McDowall, David, "A Profile of the Population of the West Bank and Gaza Strip". In:*Journal of Refugee Studies* (1989), pp. 20–26.

Milton-Edwards, Beverly, *Islamic Politics in Palestine*, (London, 1996).

Milton-Edwards, Beverly, "Political Islam in an Environment of Peace?", in: *Third World Quarterly*, Vol. 17, no. 2, (1996), pp. 199–225.

Mitchell, Richard P. , *The Society of the Muslim Brothers*, (London, 1969).

Monshipouri, M, "The PLO Rivalry with Hamas – The Challenge of Peace, Democratisation and Islamic Radicalism". In: *Middle East Policy*, 4 (1996), pp. 84–105).

Nettler, Ronald, *Past Trials and Present Tribulations. A Muslim Fundamentalist View of the Jews*, (Oxford, 1987).

Nettler, Ronald (ed), *Studies in Muslim Jewish Relations*, vol. 1, (Harwood Academic Publishers, Amsterdam, 1993).

Nettler,Ronald, "Arab Images of Jews and Israel", in: *Survey of Jewish Affairs*, Oxford 1989, pp. 33–43.

Peretz, Don, *Intifada: The Palestinian Uprising*, (Boulder, 1990).

Peretz, Don, "Secular-Religious Tension within the Palestinian Resistance Movement". In: *Middle East Focus*, Fall 1990, Vol. 12 (3), pp. 13–17.

Peters, Rudolph, "Erneuerungsbewegungen im Islam vom 18. bis 20. Jahrhundert und die Rolle des Islams in der neueren Geschichte: Antikolonialismus und Nationalismus". In: Ende/Steinbach (eds), *Der Islam in der Gegenwart*, (München, 1984), pp. 91–132.

Peters, Rudolph, *Jihad in Medieval and Modern Islam*, (Leiden, 1977).

Peters, Rudolph, *Islam and Colonialism. The Doctrine of Jihad in Modern History*, (The Hague, 1979).

Piscatori, James P., *Islam in a World of Nation-States*, (Cambridge, 1986).

Piscatori, James P. (ed), *Islamic Fundamentalisms in the Gulf Crisis*, (Chicago, 1991).

Qutb, Muḥammad, "Introduction" to Sayyid Qutb, *In the Shade of the Qur'ān*, vol. 30, (London, 1979).

Qutb, Sayyid, *Ma'ālim fī l-Ṭarīq*, 13th edition, (Cairo, 1989).

Qutb, Sayyid, *Al-'Adāla al-Ijtimā'iyya fī l-Islām*, 4th edition, (Cairo, 1954).

Qutb, Sayyid, *Fī Ẓ.ilāl al-Qur'ān*, (Beirut, 1982).

Rashad, Ahmad, *Hamas: Palestinian Politics with an Islamic Hue*, (Springfield VA, December 1993), Occasional Paper Series no. 2.

Reissner, Johannes, "Die militant-islamischen Gruppen". In: Ende/Steinbach (eds), *Der Islam in der Gegenwart*, (München, 1984), pp. 470–487.

Roberts, Adam, "The Palestinians, The Uprising, and International Law", p. 33. In: *Journal for Refugee Studies (1989)*, pp. 26–40.

Roberts, Hugh, "A Trial of Strength: Algerian Islamism". in: Piscatori, *Islamic Fundamentalisms in the Gulf Crisis*, (Chicago 1991), pp. 131–153.

Roy, Sarah, "The Gaza Strip: Critical Effects of the Occupation." In: Aruri, *Occupation*, pp. 249–295.

Roy, Sarah, *The Gaza Strip. Political Development of De-Development*, (Washington, 1995)

Saad Eddin Ibrahim, "Anatomy of Egypt's Militant Islamic Groups: Methodological note and Preliminary Findings", in: *International Journal for Middle East Studies*, 12 (1980), pp. 423–453.

Saad Eddin Ibrahim, "An Islamic Alternative in Egypt: The Muslim Brotherhood and Sadat", in: *Arab Studies Quarterly*, Vol. 4, No. 1&2, 1982, pp. 75–93.

Said, Edward W., "Symbols versus Substance: A Year after the Declaration of Principles", Interviewed by Mouin Rabbani in *Journal of Palestine Studies*, no. 2 (Winter 1995), pp. 60–72

Satloff, Robert, "Islam in the Palestinian Uprising". In: *Policy Focus*, 7 (October 1988).

Schiff, Ze'ev and Ya'ari, Ehud, *Intifada: The Palestinian Uprising. Israel's third front*, (New York, 1990).

Sivan, Emmanuel, *Radical Islam. Medieval Theology and Modern Politics*, (New Haven, 1985).

Sivan, Emmanuel and Friedman, Menachem (eds), *Religious Radicalism & Politics in the Middle East*, (Albany, 1990).

Shadid, Mohammad K., "The Muslim Brotherhood Movement in the West Bank and Gaza". In: *Third World Quarterly*, 10/2 (1988), pp. 658–682.

Smith, Wilfred Cantwell Smith, *Islam in Modern History*, (Princeton, 1957).

Taraki, Lisa, "The Islamic Resistance Movement in the Palestinian Uprising". In: Zachary Lockman/Joel Beneinin (eds), *Intifada,* pp. 171–182.

Taraki, Lisa, "The Islamic Resistance Movement in the Palestinian Uprising", *Middle East Report*, 156 (1989), pp. 30–32.

Taraki, Lisa, "Mass Organisations in the West Bank". In: Aruri, *Occupation*, pp. 431–463.

Tibi, Bassam, *Der Islam und das Problem der kulturellen Bewältigung Sozialen Wandels*, paperback, (Frankfurt, 1985).

Usher, Graham, "What Kind of a Nation? The Rise of *Ḥamās* in the Occupied Territories". In: *Race and Class*, 37, (1995), pp. 65–80.

Vatikiotis, P. J., *Islam and the State*, (London, 1987).

Watt, W. Montgomery, *Islamic Political thought. The Basic Concepts*, (Edinburgh, 1968).

Watt, W. Montgomery, *Islamic Fundamentalism and Modernity*, (London, 1988).

Zubaida, Sami, *Islam, the People and the State*, (London, 1989).

Zubaida, Sami, "Islam, Cultural Nationalism and the Left". In: *Review of Middle East Studies*, 4 (1988), pp. 1–32.

Index